THE SALES STAR

THE SALES STAR

A Real-World Story of Sales Success

The companion guide to
Buyer-Approved Selling:
Sales Secrets from the Buyer's Side of the Desk

MICHAEL SCHELL

Approved Publications Inc.

The Sales Star: A Real-World Story of Sales Success

Senior Editor: Andy Fielding

Associate Editors: Eva Nerelius, Åsa Nerelius, Mark Bourgeois, Mitch Merker

Published by **Approved Publications Inc.**
Suite 208 - 700 West Pender Street
Vancouver, British Columbia
V6C 1G8

Call us toll-free: **1-877-870-0009**
Visit our website: **www.approvedseries.com**

Second printing December 2004

National Library of Canada Cataloguing in Publication Data
Schell, Michael, 1959-
The sales star: a real world story of sales success / Mike Schell.

ISBN 0-9731675-2-1
I. Title.
PS8637.C44S34 2004 C813'.6 C2004-902779-4

Cover design: Rocks-DeHart Public Relations

Interior design: Andy Fielding

Printed in Canada

This book is dedicated with love to my wonderful grandmother, Mrs. Ruth Hannaford, a constant wealth of inspiration to me.

If I believe I cannot do something, it makes me incapable of it. But when I believe I can, then I acquire the ability to do it, even if I did not have the ability in the beginning.

– Mahatma Gandhi

If you think you can or can't do something, you're right.

– Henry Ford

Contents

Gratitude

I had a dream to write a series of books. It would have remained a dream without the inspiration, belief, unwavering support, and mind-power of many dedicated people.

Jason Foyle, valued friend, fellow musician, and fellow director of Approved Group Inc., is the original investor in the Approved Series vision and continues to motivate our team and support our collective goals.

Mitch Merker, valued friend and business partner, CEO of Marketshare Research Institute, and vice president and COO of Approved Group Inc., led the research team as they collected and analyzed the outstanding feedback in this book.

Eva Nerelius, valued friend and business operations manager of Approved Group Inc., continues to make our vision a reality with her dedication and outstanding abilities (including her editing skills).

Åsa Nerelius and Mark Bourgeois, my valued friends and two amazing members of the Approved Group Inc. executive team, always impress me with their outstanding people skills, editing acumen, and extra-mile resolve.

The incredibly talented team at Dexior Financial Inc.—especially Gerard Darmon, Sai Jiwani Mohamed, Sanja Spasojevic and Marc Poitras—contributed their valued support, inspiration, and advice. We couldn't have done it without them.

Andy Fielding, the ApprovedTM Series's Chief Editor, helped me bring this book's characters to life, and also did a fine job designing its pages.

My good friend Colin Simpson's vision, focus, and successful writing endeavors inspired me to realize my goal of becoming a writer.

Mitch Bardwell, Director and Assistant General Manager of the Sales Training Division at Canon U.S.A., Inc., took the time to read the manuscript, and wrote an excellent foreword.

Finally, my grandmother Ruth Hannaford, my mother Angela Hannaford, and my nephew Ben Schell inspired and motivated me to stay focused on this project and see it through.

To all of you, my sincere thanks!

Foreword

In Canon's Sales Training division, we have a maxim: "Knowledge shared, momentum gained." It reflects one of our ongoing priorities: to continually find *ideas that work* and provide them to our sales channels. This is one of the hallmarks of a great sales organization.

That is why, last year, we distributed copies of *Buyer-Approved Selling: Sales Strategies from the Buyer's Side of the Desk* to our entire Canon sales force. Finally, a first-hand look into the buyer's psyche, full of common-sense, real-world strategies for success—a solid framework for sales-representative behavior.

But just reading a book like *Buyer-Approved Selling* doesn't guarantee results. You've got to *live* it.

That's the purpose of this book. It takes you on a step-by-step journey through the eyes of Jack, a new rep who wants to be the best but doesn't quite know how. It's an opportunity for you to step into Jack's shoes and see how you can apply this knowledge to the art of selling—anything.

It's also about embracing the idea of serious, hard work if you want to come out on top. It says, "If you want to achieve success, work hard *now*, set your goals *now*, put your systems and behaviors in place *now*."

It's one thing to learn something, and another to apply it. This book will help you do both. It demystifies what it takes to be a top salesperson.

MITCH BARDWELL
DIRECTOR & ASSISTANT GENERAL MANAGER
SALES TRAINING DIVISION, CANON U.S.A., INC.

Introduction

After the success of Buyer-Approved Selling, I felt that a companion guide in the form of a real-world story was required. In the spirit of the research behind *Buyer-Approved Selling*, I asked many people if they thought this story concept made sense. Their answer was a resounding "Yes!" So off I went to the sunny shores of Jamaica, where I found a beautiful and inspiring spot to focus on writing.

People who work in the unforgiving business world need knowledge that is practical, not theoretical. I created real-world scenarios for Jack, my sales-rep character, where he could apply the knowledge in *Buyer-Approved Selling*—and this book came to life.

The situations Jack encounters reflect the reality of today's corporate sales. He finds himself in a world where he and his fellow sales reps are given an unusual amount of free reign. With no managers breathing down his neck or holding his hand, Jack is free to be his best ally or his worst enemy. He soon learns that success is all about choice—in particular, the choice to form winning habits.

Like Jack, I have held various commission-based, corporate sales positions. I worked for a company very similar to BigCo, with over 70 sales reps. I saw a first-year rep close a major deal that earned him nine months of quota and a commission that exceeded the average rep's annual earnings. I mention these things because it's important for you, the reader, to know how real this story can be.

This book can help you visualize a winning future for yourself. It's simply a matter of following Jack and Morena's lead. Grab a copy of *Buyer-Approved Selling* and customize the sales "secrets" to your own selling situation. As long as the products or services you sell offer true value, and you follow the Buyer-Approved approaches consistently and with integrity, you can't lose. That's right—*you can't lose!*

Think of all the sales reps who will never read *Buyer-Approved Selling* or *The Sales Star*. They will never benefit from the hundreds of buyers who have shared their winning approaches on how to sell to them. If those reps aren't doing it, and you are—well, need I say more?

Enjoy the read. I wish you all the best as you distinguish yourself from the masses and earn more business.

Chapter 1
Jack's Orientation

Jack Fontaine pulled his beat-up 1992 Mustang into the parking lot of BigCo, his new employer. He turned off the ignition and sat there for a moment, pondering the large, modern building.

Getting through this day will be an event in itself, he thought. Sure, he was happy he'd been hired by a large, well-known company—but what were his chances of becoming a successful sales person?

Most of the sales people Jack knew were outgoing, magnetic, life-of-the-party types. That certainly didn't describe him. He was the quiet, dependable type. Factor in a healthy dose of impatience, and that pretty much described him. He considered himself an average-looking guy—five foot ten, 165 pounds, brown eyes, brown hair. He ate well, worked out regularly, played hockey now and then, and on a good day he might get a look or two from the ladies. But Mr. Charismatic, Mr. Outgoing? No way.

So what am I doing here? Am I really about to walk in and become a sales rep?

The position was commission-heavy, but the company claimed that the average rep with a year or more of tenure earned $60,000 per year; top reps made $150K-plus. That was way better than Jack could get elsewhere.

Well, I've come this far—I'll give it my best shot. He got out and walked through the front doors of BigCo to meet his new colleagues. It was November 1, a Friday. Normally, it'd be a strange day to start a new job—but not in sales, where performance was tracked from the beginning of each month to its end.

Look good, feel good, and deliver better results

BigCo Inc. was a large, publicly-traded company with offices throughout the U.S. They'd advertised three new outside corporate sales positions with complete training. As Jack walked into BigCo's opulent reception area, he wondered once again how he'd landed the job.

"Hi, I'm Jack Fontaine," Jack told the receptionist. "I'm here for Bart Thomas." Bart was Jack's new sales manager.

Jack wasn't a successful sales rep yet, but he looked the part. At first, he'd hesitated to invest in a new business wardrobe. Then he'd read Napoleon Hill's advice about the psychology of good clothes, and he'd decided they'd be a wise investment in his future. So, before he started interviewing, he'd carefully shopped for some quality suits, dress shirts, ties, and a new watch, belt, and shoes. He'd even picked up a Mont Blanc fountain pen and a leather business case.

Napoleon Hill said that dressing well was about more than impressing other people. It had a profound effect on the person wearing the clothes. Although he'd spent more than he'd planned, Jack felt it was worth it—he felt like a million.

He must have looked good to BigCo too—they were only the eighth company to interview him. But Jack had done his research. Corporate sales was competitive, and there was a lot of turnover. At any time, one-third of all reps were rookies of 90 days or fewer; another third were on their way out; and the remaining third were the vets, the "shooters."

Jack's new attire made him feel confident, but they couldn't turn him into the aggressive, slick-talking deal-maker he figured BigCo was looking for. He wondered: *Will I even make it through the three-month probation period?*

Neighborly advice

Then Bart, his new boss, was standing in front of him. "Hello, Jack," he said with a warm smile and a firm handshake.

"Hi, Bart—how's your day going?" Jack's neighbor, a retired G.E. executive, had told him, "When you meet someone in business, don't say 'How are you?' It sounds insincere. You've just met the person, and it's a business setting. That's exactly what you expect a sales rep to say."

"Glad you asked, Jack," said Bart as they walked down the hall. "Because it's a little crazy right now. A top prospect is coming in for a last-minute presentation. It's our final shot, so I need to be there. I thought I'd leave you with Jason—he's been here five years and he can get you up to speed. We'll meet again after the presentation."

The Sales Pit

They entered an area with a dozen desks where several people were working. Jack could see Bart's office across the hall. "Here we are," Bart said, "your new home—the Sales Pit. And here's Jason. He'll introduce you to the rest of the team." As Jack and Jason shook hands, Bart said, "Now you'll have to excuse me. See you in a while."

Jason radiated confidence. He seemed like someone who got what he wanted out of life—the kind of person who dove in and made things happen. "I think you'll like working for BigCo, Jack," he said. "We're high-energy, we have tons of team spirit, and we're not afraid to try new things. And BigCo doesn't hesitate to show its gratitude to top performers."

He took Jack around the Sales Pit and introduced him to the other members of the team. Each of them greeted Jack warmly—until he was introduced to Grant. As Grant took Jack's hand, he brashly pushed Jack back against a desk. "How's it going, buddy?" Grant said, without smiling. "Before you get started, there's something you should know: The last three reps who tried to make it on our team—they didn't make it. Anyhow, I'd like to stick around and chat, but I have deals to close." He picked up his case and walked briskly away.

"Don't let him get to you. He's a good guy, but a little arrogant at times. He doesn't take to rookies. See, Jack, we're the top sales team in the company, and we expect a lot from ourselves. Well, I'd better hit the road myself. If there's anything I can do for you, let me know. Welcome to the team!"

Jack went over to his desk to wait for Bart to return. He looked at some sales brochures. What had he gotten himself into? And what the heck was up with that Grant character? He'd give an aspirin a headache.

Sink or swim

Jack was in Bart's office, discussing his new job. "A neighbor of mine was an exec at G.E.," Jack said. "You could call him my mentor. He told me, 'Learn from existing excellence, or invent mediocrity.' So before I start doing my own sales calls, are you going to send me out to watch some of your experienced reps?"

"We tried that for a while, but it didn't work. No one wants to baby-sit a new rep—we're too busy. So it's a sink-or-swim deal. If you're a self-starter, you have what it takes. Monday morning you'll begin our four-day training. That should show you everything you need to know."

"Whatever you say," said Jack. He smiled, hoping the sinking feeling in his stomach didn't show on his face.

"Okay, you'd better get moving. You need to be at orientation in five minutes. Go down the hall to the front office, turn left, and look for Human Resources. It's the first door on the right."

A human connection

"If you're Jack," said the woman at Human Resources, "I'll have to ask you to take a seat for a few minutes."

Jack sat down, and she continued. "You'll be meeting with Vivian, our HR manager—but she's running a bit late. Two of you are scheduled for 9:30 . . . Oh, this may be our other person right here. Are you Morena?"

"That's me." A smiling young woman had entered the room. She had thick, wavy shoulder-length brown hair, and big blue eyes. Her warm, engaging smile and sparkling eyes suggested that she wasn't the type to put on airs or act conceited.

"You're right on time. Unfortunately, Vivian is running just a few minutes late today. Just take a seat with Jack and we'll get you started soon."

"Hi, Jack," said Morena, offering her hand. After twenty minutes of conversation, Jack felt he and Morena were kindred spirits. She was authentic, sincere, and had such positive energy. True, she was a bit talkative—but that didn't bother Jack, who preferred to let others do the talking. Only his first day on the job, and it seemed like he was already making his first real friend.

The company tour

"Characters—that's one way to describe them," said Vivian as she lead Jack and Morena to Customer Service. "Yes, you have some interesting personalities over there in Sales. And I must say, you guys have it made—you have so much autonomy. It's nothing like HR, where I'm glued to one spot most of the day."

"As you may know, Jack, some of our top reps are on your team—and I can tell you there's no lack of ego there. They really do think they're quite special. And I guess they are, considering we have seventy-three sales reps here. When you're on top, ego must be part of the package."

Jack knew that if he were the number-one rep, it would be different. He'd never forgotten his neighbor's words: "A good leader praises others when things go right, and accepts the blame when things go wrong. Humility is the key."

"Now, Morena," Vivian was saying, "your teammates are colorful, too. Not like Jack's—but this business is so competitive, it takes a certain kind of person to succeed. If you survive your 90-day probation, you'll pick up quite a bit of business savvy. Some of our former reps have gone on to great things."

Vivian was colorful herself, Jack thought. They could have put her on the sales team instead of him.

"Okay, folks, here we are," said Vivian. "We'll be chatting with Martin, our customer service manager, about how his team helps us keep customers long enough to sell them our next version of software. Then we'll visit the admin manager, then Tech Support . . ."

Shouldn't all customers be treated equally?

The orientation was finished by mid-afternoon. Jack stopped by Bart's office to see what was next, but he wasn't in. So he went back to his desk in the Sales Pit. At the next desk sat Garrett, one of his fellow reps. He was just hanging up his phone, a big grin on his face.

"Work smart or work hard—that's what they say, right? But man, a deal like that is like catching apples falling off a tree. The guy calls in, and right away he knows what he wants—he used our hardware and software at the last company he worked for. And *wham*, there's 75% of my month's quota! Get this, too: He bought it at *list*—30% more than the promotion we've been running."

"Is that for real?" Jack said. "Does the company really let us decide what prices to give customers?"

"Absolutely. It's a tough job, and the company gives us a lot of flexibility on closings. Sometimes, when there's competition, we have to ask Bart to let us give discounts, and that knocks down our commissions. So when I get a chance to sell something at full list—I'm on it, baby!"

"What if the customer talks to somebody else, and they find out they paid 30% more than they had to? Isn't that a problem?"

"Nah," said Garrett. "I'd just tell them that with all the products we carry and all the promotions we do, I got a little confused. And I'd just credit them, and give up some of my commission. But they never call back like that—it's never happened to me. Well, I better get this order over to admin. Then I need to bail out early today—got some things going on!"

"Exciting times at BigCo right now, Jack," Bart said with a smile. "Your timing couldn't be better. We're launching our biggest sales contest ever—and that's saying a lot. This industry is known for good incentive programs for sales reps. Last year, the reps and sales managers who made quota went on a first-class Caribbean cruise. The year before, it was Paris. And this year, it's a nine-day trip—five days in Hawaii and four in Acapulco.

"But listen, Jack, I'd better explain how your commissions are calculated. Once a sales rep reaches their monthly quota, they get an extra 3% over and above the 12% base commission. When they reach their quarterly quota, they earn an extra 2% on their total sales for the quarter. And finally, if they make their annual quota, they get an extra 1% bonus on their annual sales.

"That really adds up. Our reps average fifty to sixty thousand a year. Some of the reps on our team—the top team—are pulling in over $150,000. And one year, one of our reps earned over $180,000 and a first-class trip for two to St. Lucia."

Jack left Bart's office feeling elated. He couldn't believe the opportunity that lay before him. Talk about motivation! There were lots of reasons to treat this like his own business rather than just a job. Of course he'd also asked Bart about the low-income numbers. For every rep who earned six figures a year, there were nine others who were making five—some as low as $30,000. It was like his neighbor said: "Always identify and examine the flip-side of every business decision."

VIP parking available

As he walked out to the parking lot, Jack bumped into Morena. "How's it going, Jack?" she said. "Did you enjoy the rest of the day?"

"Absolutely. Did your manager tell you how we could earn a nice fat six-figure income, as well as a free first-class trip to Hawaii *and* Acapulco?"

"She sure did. Acapulco is okay—but I've always wanted to go to Hawaii."

"Well, I'm going to both," said Jack, "and I'd better see you there too!"

"Okay, you talked me into it," Morena laughed.

At that moment, a shiny new silver BMW pulled out of a parking space beside the main entrance, revealing a sign that said SALES PERSON OF THE MONTH.

"When I win that," said Jack, "I hope I have a better car than the one I'm driving now."

"What are you driving now?"

"An old Mustang—and it's had its day."

"Don't feel bad. I'm not even going to tell you what I get around in—but it's old, beat-up, and it rhymes with 'Minto'."

As they walked, it started to rain. "Oh no," said Morena. "My car is way over on the other side of the lot, and I don't have an umbrella."

"Here," said Jack, "Share mine. But this means I'm going to find out what you're driving!" And off they walked, through the rain, across the huge parking lot.

As it rained harder, a vivid image entered Jack's mind: He was leaving the office after another successful day. It was raining, but he didn't care—he had to walk only a few feet to the spot that said SALES PERSON OF THE MONTH, where he opened the door of his brand-new car.

That morning, Jack had worried he wouldn't make it as a sales rep. Now he was seeing himself as *top* rep! Was he getting carried away? Now that he'd met his manager and team members, he felt something changing inside him. *If they can do this job and make the big bucks, I can, too.*

Chapter 2
Diving Into the Deep End

★

All the new BigCo sales reps received an intense four-day training at the company's main training center, 50 miles from Jack's office. To qualify for a sales position with BigCo, you had to complete the training with a grade of at least 80% on the product knowledge exam—and there were no exceptions.

Eight enthusiastic, outgoing new reps were flown in from other regional offices to take part in the training. Jack and Morena soon realized they were the quietest two personalities in the group. Again, Jack wondered if he was cut out for the job.

The first two days of the training focused on the company's products. Jack and Morena found the information easy to understand. Nonetheless, they spent time each evening reviewing the day's material until they felt they had mastered it.

The last two days, Wednesday and Thursday, were devoted to sales techniques. Then, before Jack and Morena knew it, it was Thursday afternoon and time for the crucial product-knowledge exam.

"Let's take a ten-minute break before we start the exam," the instructor said, as he wrapped up the final training module.

"Only one thing bothers me," Jack said to Morena. "They taught us a lot about how to sell *to* a buyer—but what about seeing things from the buyer's perspective? Isn't that important?"

"You're right, Jack. A lot of the training made sense, but a lot of it seemed to gloss over key areas. I know we're here to learn the BigCo approach to sales, but I'm not sure how I feel about everything they taught us. Oh well, the break's over—let's go ace that exam!"

Jack's and Morena's extra study paid off—they each scored over 90%. They felt confident that they could represent BigCo competently and knowledgeably, even if they were a little skeptical about some of the stilted sales approaches they'd learned.

"We'll do the best we can with it," said Jack, "and we'll see how we do."

Jack's first call

Friday brought rain, and it was hard for Jack to get out of bed that morning. The coffee helped, but he was weary from the last four days of intense study and training. Maybe he'd get to relax a bit when he reached the office.

But it was not to be. No sooner had he reached his desk than he heard his direct line ringing with the special sound that indicated an external call.

"Good morning, Jack Fontaine," he said, as cheerfully as his foggy brain would allow.

"Hello, Jack," said a businesslike voice. "This is Frank Mitchell at BuyerCo Industries. We're shopping for an entry-level system. I've met with two vendors, but our policy is to get three quotes before we acquire any new equipment. I'd like to see someone from BigCo as soon as possible. Any chance we could meet this afternoon?"

"That shouldn't be a problem, Frank. I'll see if I can rearrange a couple of things, and I'll get right back to you."

Jack went to Bart's office and told him the news. He assumed Bart or one of the other reps would be going on the call with him.

But Bart said, "Sorry Jack, I can't help you on this one. I'm in meetings all day. The rest of the team is tied up too. You'll have to dive into the deep end alone this time. But don't worry, you have some excellent training under your belt now. Call that prospect back and set an appointment for this afternoon. Don't worry, you'll be fine."

Jack meets Frank

New suit or not, Jack was apprehensive as he drove to his first sales call. He mentally reviewed the selling techniques he'd been taught in his BigCo training. "People buy from people they like," the trainer said. "It's crucial to establish rapport with your prospect as soon as possible." How could Jack pull that off? He wasn't one of those pump-your-hand, "how-ya-doing" kinds of guys. Well, he'd just do the best he could.

When Jack entered Frank Mitchell's office, he smiled, introduced himself, and shook Frank's hand. "Thanks for having me in today, Frank," he said.

"Have a seat, Jack," Frank said, indicating a chair by his desk.

So far, so good.

As Jack sat down, he took a quick look at the photos on Frank's desk. He immediately spotted one of Frank in a fishing outfit, proudly holding a large pike. *All right,* thought Jack—*I know about fishing.* He'd spent some happy summers at his Uncle Joe's cottage on Lake Newaygo. Those were the days—no responsibilities, no work, no stressful sales calls . . .

"Where did you land that beauty?" Jack asked—and so began the Rapport-Building Stage. Frank and Jack spent the next twenty minutes chatting about all the fishing they'd done.

Jack started to relax. Frank seemed to be enjoying the conversation. But how could Jack steer him toward business, so he could start telling him about BigCo systems? He started getting nervous again.

A minute later, Frank solved the problem for him. He looked at the clock and said, "Wow, I had no idea how late it was. I'll have to wrap this up in a few minutes. What do you have for me?"

Yikes! Jack thought. How could he make his whole presentation in a few minutes? There was no time for the qualifying and "pain-building" questions BigCo's trainers had taught them. He jumped right into his presentation, and his carefully-planned meeting structure went out the window. Before he knew it, he was pulling out glossy brochures, sheets about BigCo's achievements, testimonial letters, and color photocopies of industry awards.

As Jack spoke, Frank listened and nodded. Jack wondered if he should ask Frank some questions about his particular needs, or if he had any questions for Jack. But Frank had requested the brochures, and he was reading each document as Jack handed it to him. So Jack carried on, speaking glowingly about the quality, reliability, and low operating costs of BigCo systems.

Ten minutes later, Frank said, "Okay, Jack, I think I have all the information I need. Let me put a report together for our VP of finance and I'll get back to you sometime next week."

Wow! Was it Jack's imagination, or was Frank saying he was practically ready to order? This sales stuff wasn't so hard after all!

"Okay, Frank. Thanks for your time. Just let me know if there's anything else I can do for you." They chatted a bit more about fishing as they strolled back to the lobby.

Jack grinned as he made his way back to his car. That trainer was right: People buy from people they like. Jack and Frank had gotten along great, and all of those BigCo sales materials spoke for themselves. *I think I just made my first sale! Not a bad way to end the week. Bart will be impressed.*

Just then there was a loud thunderclap, and rain pelted down on him. He ran to his beat-up Mustang, hopped in, and began the trip home. It was 5 P.M.

Chapter 3
Buyer-Approved Selling

"How's it going, neighbor?" Jack called. The rain had stopped soon after he'd gotten home, and he'd spotted his neighbor through the kitchen window.

"Well, I'm still on the right side of the grass, Jack—that's a plus. So tell me, how'd your day go?"

"Let's see—do you have an hour to spare?" Jack smiled. He told his neighbor about the sales and product training, and how his first sales call looked like it would be his first sale. He told his neighbor about Morena, and how compatible he felt they'd be as coworkers.

"Sounds great, Jack. I'd like to hear more, but I'm going out for dinner tonight and I have to get ready. I do have a question, though: Now that you've gotten a look at BigCo, are you going to give the selling profession a serious shot?"

"You bet I am—my best shot!"

"That's good to hear, Jack, because I may have some new information for you that will help you do just that. I'm meeting a contact for dinner, and if what he says is true, I'll have something for you that will show you how to become a master sales communicator. I can give it to you tomorrow morning, if you're around."

"That sounds pretty exciting."

"It is. Well, I'd better get going. See you later!"

The neighbor comes through

It was Saturday. Jack walked out into his backyard and saw his neighbor relaxing on his deck.

"This is your lucky day!" he said as Jack approached. "My contact delivered the goods. Here are copies of a brand-new book for you and your friend Morena—a book that will show you, step-by-step, how to conduct Buyer-Approved sales interactions with confidence."

He handed the books to Jack. They were called *Buyer-Approved Selling: Sales Secrets from the Buyer's Side of the Desk.*

"This is a whole new concept in sales training, Jack. It's a complete rundown of the sales process, with tips specifically approved by professional buyers. It even includes the buyers' actual comments about the things reps do, the things they don't do, and the things they *wish* they'd do. It's a real eye-opener."

Jack looked at the back cover. There were endorsements from a VP at Oracle, and from Canon U.S.A.'s director of sales training. He scanned the first few pages. The foreword was written by the global lead buyer at DaimlerChrysler.

"Wow," said Jack. "I read three sales books before my interview at BigCo, but they were really subjective—nothing like this. Where did you say you got these?"

"I know the national sales manager for one of the major electronics companies. He liked the book so much that he bought copies for all of his reps. He's been introducing the author to people in his industry and helping him develop customized corporate editions. He had some extra copies for me in exchange for some ideas I shared with him.

"I'm telling you, Jack, this book is the real deal. When my colleague told me about it, I immediately thought about you and

Morena. I couldn't think of a better way to use these copies than to promote your careers."

"Thanks very much," said Jack, shaking his neighbor's hand. "I'm going to read mine right now, while I have dinner."

He walked back to the house. Asking buyers what worked for them—it made such sense. He was looking forward to this.

It's all about the buyer

It took Jack only an hour and a half to read *Buyer-Approved Selling*—but it took Marketshare Research Institute nearly two years to get the opinions of over 200 professional buyers across the U.S., in a wide range of industries, to form the basis of the book. They'd asked the buyers questions about all aspects of sales, including:

- Which sales approaches they liked, and why
- How much each approach influenced their decisions
- How many sales reps used these successful approaches

There was a clear, step-by-step description of each approved method, with a wealth of actual comments from the buyers. It even included charts showing the buyers' overall responses, and planning guides for customizing the techniques.

But what Jack found most interesting was this: Although the buyers agreed on many techniques reps could use to get more sales, *most reps didn't use them.* Most of the reps didn't even seem *aware* of them.

That had made Jack pause. He hadn't used any of these approaches with Frank on Friday. But somehow, they'd still had a great meeting. He guessed that Frank must have liked him enough not to care.

Jack re-read several sections of the book that he found most interesting, and finally put it down at 10 P.M. It was all so direct and practical—real-world stuff. If he could use these techniques properly and consistently, he could make a *lot* of money. He could do it by helping people get what they needed, selling to them the way they wanted to buy.

Though it was late, Jack called Morena. He was too excited to wait. "That sounds a lot better than what they taught us in sales training class," she said. "Why do all that guesswork, when you can hear what works from the buyer's side of the desk?"

"Exactly," Jack said. "No kidding, Morena—if we use this material, I think we really have a fighting chance."

"Sounds like we have more than that," she said. "I'd say we're on our way to some knockouts!"

Practice beats theory

The next morning, Jack couldn't wait to get started. He reexamined the book's tips over breakfast and started thinking about how he could adapt them to his work at BigCo.

For cold calls, the book said it was important that sales reps prepare industry-specific *Key Point Statements* so they could present their initial information clearly and concisely. When the rep spoke with the prospect, the book recommended that the rep *ask for the prospect's permission to proceed,* rather than just charging ahead with the call. The buyers said that showed respect for their time, and that it raised their respect for the rep. Get to the point quickly, the buyers advised; state your point succinctly, and use common courtesy.

Plan your work, work your plan

Jack knew from experiences that a road map was essential for the success of any enterprise. At university, he'd worked on several team projects that hadn't been finished by their deadlines. When he analyzed them, he was sure they would have succeeded if the team had written out clear goals and completion dates.

To improve his skills in that area, Jack took a seminar on designing written "game plans" for goals. His goal was to earn at least $100,000 a year—as some of the people on his sales team were doing now.

If they can do it, I can too.

Jack called Morena. "Morena, what would you think about collaborating on a one-year plan? Between the two of us, and the techniques in *Buyer-Approved Selling,* I think we could create detailed goals that we could meet, and probably exceed."

"Sounds great!" said Morena. "Got some time? We could get started right now, over the phone."

"Let's go," said Jack. "May I switch you to my speakerphone, so I can write?"

"Sure. I'll do the same with you."

They got to work outlining their three initial goal areas:

- Cold calls
- Appointments
- Proposals

They planned how many of each they would commit to each week, and how they would achieve them.

An hour later, they felt as though they were gaining control over their new careers—that they had a clear sense of direction.

"How about lunch tomorrow?" Morena asked. "We could meet at that coffee shop on 21st Avenue, next to the library."

"Sounds good to me."

Having information isn't the same as using it

As Jack drove to the coffee shop, he considered how simple the *Buyer-Approved Selling* principles were. You didn't need to be an expert to customize, practice, and use them. And what a competitive advantage! But he could understand why a lot of reps wouldn't bother with them: They took extra time and work. The guys at BigCo were always complaining about how little time they had. It was ironic—but Jack knew that if they used the techniques, they'd be more efficient, and they'd have *more* time.

As Jack pulled into the parking lot, he imagined he was BigCo's top sales rep pulling into the coveted parking space next to the president's. Jack's team called him "The Rookie." Well, he'd enjoy seeing their faces when he grabbed the number-one spot.

He saw Morena getting out of her car. He honked and waved.

"Did you bring the book?"

"Here you go," said Jack, handing over her copy.

"I'm sending your neighbor a handwritten thank-you card. There's just not enough handwritten mail these days."

"Agreed—you can't go wrong with handwritten mail. I'm sure my neighbor will appreciate it."

Data – order = chaos

Morena read the book's first tip: *Organize and manage your prospect database for maximum results.*

"That's a good way to maximize the time you spend converting prospects to customers," she said. "So how come we don't do that at BigCo? We're an established company, yet we have no set system for our sales reps to use when working their territories. The tips in this book aren't rocket science, and all these buyers say they're conducive to the sale. But from what I'm reading, it seems that most companies don't use them."

"I wonder if they would, if they knew how strongly buyers felt about them?"

"Speaking of efficiency, Jack—you should see the data file my manager gave me yesterday. What a mess! Just sorted alphabetically, with no priority sorting at all. The last rep who used it never even bothered to update it."

"Same thing happened to me," Jack said. He pointed to a page in the book. "It says to sort your data by industry type, if you have enough types to warrant it. I was checking out my territory file, and I have a lot of insurance companies, legal firms, and accounting firms."

"Join the club," said Morena, "I have a bunch of manufacturing plants, too."

"Looks like we've found our next task."

The cost of freedom

Freedom, thought Jack—it was so important to him. Yet there he was, chained to a computer while his friends were out playing golf and enjoying the beautiful Sunday afternoon.

But when he became the top rep at BigCo, he'd have lots of freedom. As long as he kept bringing in those big numbers, he could come and go as he pleased. That's how it was in sales; he'd seen it at BigCo.

The phone rang. It was Morena.

"Think about it, Jack. Here we are, fresh out of university, and we're working for a well-known company where every transaction in our territory earns us a healthy commission!"

"That's the way I see it, too" said Jack. "It's very much like owning our own businesses. In fact, it's even better: We have the resources of a national corporation behind us, with a reputation for a quality brand. We have no cash-flow challenges, administration nightmares, or accounting to take care of—other than cashing our own pay-checks and commissions. We can put all of our time and energy into developing and serving our customers. So hey, if I need to do a little extra work here and there, it's no problem. When you get to be your own boss, you have to do what's best for the business."

Jack's first sales meeting

Jack arrived at the weekly Monday-morning meeting wondering what he would learn from it.

Bart opened the meeting by officially introducing Jack as the new team member. A few announcements were next. Then Bart asked each rep for their current monthly numbers and sales forecasts. He methodically wrote everything on a flip chart: company name, product, estimated percentage of success, total dollar value. Then he called on Jack.

Jack felt his face flush with excitement as he forecasted his first sale. But then the meeting continued to plod along, and he could feel the energy slipping out of the room.

He thought of his previous job—a summer job while he was in university. He was on a seven-member team with a major project: the company's annual sales and marketing conference, which was held in a different city each year.

Leanne, the team's leader, was an amazing organizer and manager. When the company had a complicated project with a deadline, she usually got it. Jack learned a lot from her in those four months.

It was Leanne's policy for the team members to take turns leading meetings, and Jack got to lead five of them. She taught him how to design and organize effective meetings. They'd found many ways to leverage the team's collective mind power.

Bart was finally wrapping things up. The meeting had seemed like such a waste of time. Instead of just reporting their own activities, how much information could they have shared to help all of them sell better?

Objection!

Frustration washed over Jack as he sat in his manager's office. In *Buyer-Approved Selling,* he'd read about the importance of anticipating prospects' objections and using them as an opportunity to present positive information. But when he described the method to Bart, and asked him what the top five objections were to BigCo's products and services, Bart responded negatively. "Bringing up objections on behalf of the customer? That's harmful and unnecessary. You're just asking for trouble."

Jack wanted to show Bart how highly the buyers had rated the technique. But he knew it was too much, too soon. The only way Jack could show Bart the value of the Buyer-Approved methods was to put them to work. He was more determined than ever.

With 72 other sales reps in the company, and a management that resisted new ideas, Jack's work was cut out for him. So if *Buyer-Approved Selling* was his and Morena's secret, all the more power to them. Besides, even if the other reps on their teams did have the book, he doubted most of them would bother to use it.

The VP of Sales: The Dark Side appears

Pressure and negative energy—the man radiated it. Jack had heard a lot about Herman, the vice president of sales, and it wasn't good. His arrogant, dictatorial style was legend around the office. Some of Jack's team said that the company committed self-sabotage the day they promoted Herman. Now here he was, strolling around the Sales Pit, a sour expression on his face.

"You're our new fellow, aren't you?"

"Yes, Jack Fontaine. Glad to meet you, Herman."

"How's everything going so far? Things starting to make sense for you yet?"

"You bet," said Jack. "I finished the training program Thursday. I made my first sales call Friday afternoon, and it looks like it may be my first sale."

"Well, well. I think we do a good job getting you folks up and running, don't you? I mean, considering that most of you come in off the street with no real experience, with your degrees in completely unrelated fields. You've probably heard that 33% of you don't make it past your first 90 days. But you think you may already have a sale. Well, all I can say is, good luck—you're going to need it!" And without another word, he turned and walked away.

Humble pie

So *that* was the guy in charge? Talk about a great motivator, Jack thought—how many people had he "motivated" to leave the company?

But so what? Jack's meeting with Frank was going to pay off, he was sure of it. And that was just the beginning.

As if it had been reading his thoughts, Jack's phone rang.

"Hello, Jack Fontaine."

"Frank Mitchell here, Jack."

"Great to hear from you, Frank," said Jack, remembering the good vibes they'd shared. "How's your day going?"

"Well, I'm okay, but I'm afraid I have some bad news. After our meeting on Friday, with your coming in at the last minute and all . . . I'm sorry to tell you this, but we've decided not to go with BigCo. We just signed a lease with one of your competitors."

Jack felt like his chair had been pulled out from under him. He took a breath. "May I ask why we didn't get the deal, Frank? It would be helpful to know."

"First of all, you need to know that I don't make these decisions by myself. Our VP of finance is involved on big deals like this. I meet with him after I see each rep, while the meeting is fresh in my mind. In this case, the rep who got our business brought up some things we hadn't considered, and they were crucial to our buying decision. He asked some key questions, and he prepared a meeting agenda that focused on our long-term needs.

"In fairness to you, Jack, I called him the morning before I met with you. He came in the same day, just like you did. He was very organized and thorough. He gave us confidence in his company's ability to serve us post-sale, a key criterion for us. Don't get me wrong Jack, I really enjoyed meeting with you—but in the end, business is business. I hope you understand."

Calling existing customers

Jack walked to Bart's office and told him the bad news.

"That's too bad. But there are lots of fish in the sea. And speaking of those fish, I need your help updating our customer records. A lot of critical information is missing from our files. We had a server crash last year, and we still haven't nailed everything back down. In some cases, we still need hardware model numbers as well as the software versions they're running. I know it's no fun, calling up customers and asking for information we should already have, but we've got to share the workload. Anyhow, it will give you a chance to introduce yourself as their new rep."

"Have any of the customers in my territory already been contacted? You said this problem started a year ago."

"That's right, but we've been too busy finding new orders to keep up with the old ones. You'll have to call every customer in your database—so you'd better get busy. When you're done, you can start on your monthly sales quota."

"Okay, boss," said Jack. He turned and walked back to his desk. He couldn't believe that a big company like BigCo would let things get so disorganized.

Jack met Morena for lunch and told her about the lost sale. "Don't be discouraged, Jack. *Buyer-Approved Selling* covers everything we need to do before sales calls. Let's work on customizing the methods in the book, and we'll be sales masters before we know it."

"Okay, Morena. Say, have you noticed what shape the customer records are in over in your section?"

"Yes, I'm doing the update, too," she replied. "Everyone is. Hard to believe, isn't it?"

"Did your manager give you any questions to ask your customers, other than updating their record info? I mean, as long as we'll be speaking with them?"

"None. That was a surprise, too. I wondered if you and I could come up with some good ones on our own."

"I have an idea. Why don't we ask them what their objections were before they decided to buy from us? Then we can design some Genuine Preemptive Objection Statements, as it says to do in *Buyer-Approved Selling.*"

"Good idea! Let's write some questions right now. We can use them when we make more calls after lunch."

They scripted the questions and role-played them. When lunch was over, they felt prepared, confident, and ready for some calls.

Communication mastery

"Time to improve my communications skills," said Morena as she stood in the parking lot with Jack after work. "Reading that book with all those comments from buyers gave me a new appreciation for what we say, what we don't say, and how we say it. I brought in a mini voice-recorder today to tape my side of the conversation. Then, on a break, I listened to some of the calls I made. I was not impressed!"

"May I see that? Hey, this is nice and compact. I'm going to buy one of these tonight so I can tape myself, too."

"Any chance we can get together tonight for some more role-playing? We can tape them and review them for weak words, proper intonation, and the other things the book mentions. I want to be in top shape tomorrow."

"I'm up for that," said Jack. "I need to take care of a few things first, but I can meet you at my place around 8:30."

"Perfect," said Morena. "I'll see you there. Our new goal: becoming master communicators!"

Chapter 4
Preparing for Success

Jack and Morena spent Wednesday night recording and listening to their role-plays and identifying their telephone strengths and weaknesses. Their practice session didn't end until 11:30 P.M., but the hours were well-spent. When they made more calls the next day, they agreed their performance was dramatically better.

They'd finished calling their existing customers by the end of Friday. They were ready to start calling prospects Monday morning and start generating appointments.

They met in the parking lot before heading home. "Good thing it's the weekend," said Jack. "We'll need that time to prepare our *Permission-Based Cold Call Guide.* We have to design our Key Point Statements, Industry-Specific Positioning Statements, and Primary Reason Statements. Then we'll tie them all together into a script that sounds spontaneous, rather than pre-written. So, you're sure you have enough time before Monday?"

"You bet I do," said Morena. "There's no way I'm making prospecting calls without a Buyer-Approved Cold Call Guide. Suppose we start at 10:30 Saturday morning and go till 5:00? We can work at my place this time, and I'll take care of lunch. Then, if we have more to do, we can plan for Sunday. Wow, if this weren't my own business, I'd never be working weekends!"

The kind of weekend when you want it to rain

"This Permission-Based Cold Call plan is great," Morena said. "It lets you navigate through the call step by step, with the prospect giving you permission to continue at each stage. It makes a lot more sense than bulldozing your way through."

"Asking for people's time is such a simple, courteous thing," Jack said, "It amazes me that I've never heard anyone on my sales team do it. They probably don't think about it—or if they do, maybe they're afraid they'll be turned down. But the book says that most buyers respond favorably—and if they're too busy, they often offer to reschedule the call so they can give the rep more attention."

"Okay, let's map out today's goals," Morena said. "According to the book, the first step is to create an Industry-Specific Positioning Statement. Then we need to design a Primary Reason Statement and two Key Point Statements. When that's done, we'll have what we need for our cold-call guide. The book makes it so simple. It has some great examples, too, and we can use the worksheets for customizing our material. Shall we get to work?"

The rain poured down through the day while they constructed their permission-based guide. By 5:00, their work was done, and they felt tapped-out.

"Holy mackerel!" said Jack, "There's no way I can do any more thinking. How can it be so challenging, just arranging words on a piece of paper?"

"That's why they pay copywriters the big bucks," said Morena. "It looks easy once it's done, but doing it can be a challenge! But I'm glad we took the time—it was worth it. Now, to follow it up, it would be great if we could do some role-playing tomorrow. What do you think?"

"Why don't we do that over the phone? We have our tape recorders, so we can tape our calls and review them, too."

"Great! It will save travel time—and what better way to simulate phone calls than over the phone?"

Appointment-setting: A tip from the neighbor

After Jack and Morena finished their role-plays on the telephone, Jack stepped out into his backyard for some fresh air. It was a sunny Sunday afternoon, and he was hoping he'd see his neighbor.

And there he was, lounging in his hammock. "Hello there, neighbor," he called. "Got a minute for a quick chat?"

"Always a pleasure, my friend. What's on your mind?"

"Morena and I have been working on our permission-based cold-call guides from the books you gave us. I wondered what your thoughts were on that approach."

"Yes, I read that section, and I liked it. It makes sense to ask people if they have a minute to talk, especially since you're calling them unsolicited.

"At G.E., I got calls from sales reps all the time, Jack. They'd call me out of the blue, clearly unrehearsed, stumble their way through the call, then expect me to give them an appointment! If they couldn't use one minute on the phone efficiently, why would I want to spend 20 or 30 minutes with them in person? The reps who were prepared, and who used common courtesy, always had a better chance with me. Too bad they were so rare."

"What do you think about that opening line—'Do you have a quick minute?' How do you think that would sound to most people?"

The neighbor pondered for a moment. "Well, if you call somebody who doesn't know you, and you ask for, say, five minutes of their time, you'll probably get turned down more often than not. But this 'quick minute' approach, I like it. It says the caller is sensitive about the prospect's time. That implies professionalism. And if the rest of the call is structured and to-the-point, it supports that perception."

Two cold-call approaches

Jack admitted it: Prospecting was a challenge. He made another note in his computer database. This was his eighteenth call, and that wrapped up his first calling hour. He'd been a little nervous when he started, but he'd loosened up around his seventh call and had gotten into a groove.

He couldn't imagine making effective calls with only the meager training they'd gotten the previous week. There'd been no role-playing, no recording—nothing to give the new reps any idea how they'd do under real circumstances.

He and Morena had been wise to take the time to rehearse and record themselves. They'd learned a lot. And the permission-based cold call guide they'd worked so hard to create was a great tool.

Why didn't a company with such deep pockets put more effort into developing their front-line people? What did it cost BigCo's business and reputation when their sales reps approached potential customers without research and planning? Jack knew that if it were his company, he'd never take that kind of risk.

As he worked at his desk, he listened to a couple of his teammates making cold calls. They'd been with the company for years, and they knew the company's products and services—but each call was different, without structure. He doubted that they'd ever taken the time to plan and rehearse.

Cold-calling: a "numbers game"

Jack and Morena made prospecting calls all week long. Following advice from Jack's neighbor, they booked each appointment at least five days from the day they made the call. If a sales rep seemed in a hurry, it gave the impression they weren't very busy—and therefore, weren't very successful. "Perception is reality," the neighbor said. "It's important to create the perception that you're a busy sales rep whose time is in demand."

As the week went on, they got better and better at making calls. By the end of the week, Jack had five appointments and Morena had six.

They'd booked all of their appointments for the following week. Even though they both looked forward to going on the sales calls, they knew they were in for another heavy weekend of preparation.

During their calls, They often reached decision-makers' voice mail. They'd heard their other team-members leave voice messages—but they remembered how buyers had felt about voice mail in *Buyer-Approved Selling.* What buyer had time to return 30 unsolicited messages a day, or even listen to them? When Jack and Morena couldn't reach a buyer directly, they made a note and tried again later.

"The book is right: cold-calling is a numbers game," Morena said as they walked back across the big parking lot on Friday afternoon. "I made my first appointment in my first hour Monday morning. Then there was nothing for the rest of the day, and nothing Tuesday or Wednesday. Then on Thursday I got three appointments, and two more on Friday. I guess that's why they say that 'winners never quit and quitters never win'!"

"My neighbor says that all the time," Jack chuckled. "Have you been chatting with him?"

"No, my older brother rattles off business wisdom like that all the time. He's the entrepreneur of the family, and he's done quite well. Can you say 'Porsche 911'? And then there's his beautiful lakeside estate. I want to be wealthy like he is, and I'm not afraid to work for it, either."

"You're lucky to have such a good role model."

"Well, it's important to have one—so he may as well be in my own family!"

Shouldn't everyone be singing from the same songbook?

Jack and Morena realized that they were their teams' only reps who made prospecting calls every day, even though they weren't required to. They talked about it over lunch.

"My neighbor always says, 'Business is simple; it's people that are complicated.' That's the problem. The company lets its sales reps decide what they do each day—and given a choice, most people take the path of least resistance. That means no planning, preparation, or rehearsal. And *that* means fewer calls, lower-quality calls, and fewer appointments. Nobody tries to work consistently."

"That's right, Jack. And the company wonders why there's so much turnover. Some of our territories have had four reps in the last year."

"If the company gave the reps a systematic approach like *Buyer-Approved Selling* to follow, I'm sure the reps would be more successful. They'd stick around longer, and they'd develop more lasting relationships with buyers."

"It'd make a huge difference. If everyone followed a set of common standards, we'd offer more consistency, and our customers and prospects would have a better impression of us. When people deal with a business, they like to have predictable experiences."

Making work seem less like work

"Wouldn't you know," Jack moaned to Morena on the phone, "it's a beautiful, sunny weekend, and here we are with work—lots of it. Ugh!"

"Don't bail on me, Jack. Think about Monday."

"Yeah, I know. We're going on our first Buyer-Approved sales calls, and we need to be primed."

"Hey," she said. "How about doing our work at Lake View Park on Saturday? They have benches and picnic tables. We can work with pencil and paper, and get some fresh air and sunshine."

"Now you're talking," said Jack. "By the way, Morena, I have to tell you, working with someone like you—someone who's fun to be around—makes these extra sessions go a lot easier. Thank you for that!"

"You're welcome, Jack. I can say the same about you."

Delaying gratification, investing in the future

It was Saturday morning, and a beautifully sunny day at the park. "I made a list of the things we needed to work on," Morena said. She handed it to Jack:

- __ Company information sheet
- __ Genuine Preemptive Objection Statement
- __ List of questions to ask the prospect
- __ List of questions the prospect may ask us
- __ Objective questions to leave with the prospect
- __ Advance Meeting Agenda
- __ Brief overview of BigCo that we use to open the call

"That's quite a workload," said Jack, "but I'm ready if you are."

The work was grueling. Bit by bit, they made their way through the list. The examples and worksheets in *Buyer-Approved Selling* were very helpful, but they didn't diminish the amount of thinking they had to do to create each component of the meeting planner.

As they developed the second of their three Genuine Preemptive Objection Statements, Morena turned to Jack and said, "Can you imagine doing this alone?"

"Well, it would be doable, but it's a *lot* easier to team up like this. It's like having a workout partner. It helps you stay focused, and you have someone to be accountable to. It's that old concept of one plus one making three."

When it was time for their Advance Meeting Agendas, they realized they still had to prepare them for their Monday sales calls. "I think we should send them anyway," said Morena. "I'm going to send mine from my home computer in the morning, so they'll be waiting for my prospects when they arrive at work."

"Good idea. I will, too."

It was 7:30 P.M. when they finally packed up to go home. They'd worked for ten hours, with only a few breaks and a couple of trips to the concession stand for snacks.

"Hey, do you want to see how the upper crust lives?" said Morena. "We can pop over to my brother's mansion. It's only a few minutes from here. I bet they have some real food kicking around there, too—maybe even a glass of wine. After all, it's Saturday night. We can live it up a little bit."

"Sure. I'd love to see this mansion. I could use some inspiration about now."

Can you imagine performing in a stage play without rehearsing?

"Perfect," said Jack as Morena completed her sales-meeting role-play the next day. "I really liked how you summarized the key points at the end. It was so natural, and it gave a good sense of closure. Okay, let's do them again. This time we'll videotape ourselves so we can really get a sense of how we come across."

"The meeting planner sure helps," said Morena. "I still can't believe BigCo doesn't give us these kinds of tools."

"Really," said Jack, "If it were my company, that would be different. Think about it, Morena—we haven't started our sales calls, but I bet we're a lot more prepared than most of our reps. Say, how about your research? Have you had a chance to do that yet?"

"Not yet. I need to spend some time on the Internet tonight.

This is exciting, I'm going to be so prepared for Monday. What a great feeling!"

Chapter 5
Working Toward Trust

★

Jack brimmed with confidence as he drove to his Monday-morning sales call. Thanks to the heavy rush-hour traffic, he'd gotten to listen to his rehearsal tape seven times. He felt like he could do the sales call in his sleep.

If repetition was the mother of success, then planning, preparation, and rehearsal were close cousins. It was only Jack's second sales call, but he was amazed how relaxed he was. He was usually anxious when doing something new and important. But then—hockey practice aside—he'd never spent this much time preparing for anything.

As Jack pulled into the parking lot, he realized what a good idea it had been to allow an extra 15 minutes for travel. He had exactly four minutes to get to reception, in order to be exactly one minute early for his appointment.

Appointments: Timing is everything

As Jack walked toward the entrance to his prospect's building, he recalled his neighbor's advice about being on time. "Punctuality is crucial, Jack. That means being on time—but it also means not showing up too early. Whenever possible, be at a business meeting one minute in advance. When my 11 A.M. appointment showed up at 10:45, or even 10:50. I was much too busy to rearrange my schedule on such short notice. It's safe to assume that most of the people you call on are in the same position. When you're punctual—not early, not late—you show that you stick to your plans. People like that. It builds trust."

Sorry—no second chances for first impressions

Jack walked into his potential customer's lobby. He smiled at the receptionist and said, "Good morning, I'm Jack Fontaine from BigCo. Peter King is expecting me for nine o'clock."

"Certainly, I'll tell him you're here. Please have a seat."

Peter King walked into the lobby at 9:00 sharp. "You must be Jack," he said. "Thanks for being on time. I'm on a tight schedule today."

Jack stood, smiled, and looked Peter directly in the eye while they shook hands. "Nice to meet you Peter," he said in a quiet, sincere tone, and off they went to Peter's office.

Trust + consistency + time = solid business relationships

Jack waited until Peter offered him a seat to unbutton the jacket of his new charcoal grey suit. He felt good, really good in his new threads—they were worth every penny. And he was going to translate that investment into profits from his commissions. All this raced through his mind as he took a seat.

Trust-builder #1: The AMA (Advance Meeting Agenda)

"Okay, what do you have for me?" asked Peter.

"Let me start by apologizing for sending the meeting agenda

so late. I thought I'd bring a printed copy for you, too." Jack handed Peter the brief agenda.

"Is there anything you'd like to add?"

"Not at the moment," Peter said. "Let's go ahead."

Trust-builder #2: Establish your credibility

"Before we get into the meeting," Jack said, "I thought it would be helpful if I shared a few key points about my company with you. Is that okay?"

"Go ahead."

"Thanks." Jack then did three things:

1. He gave Peter his ISPS (Industry Specific Positioning Statement) to show how BigCo could be of specific value to him.
2. He listed three of BigCo's most credible customers.
3. He shared a 20-second success story about a customer from Peter's industry who had achieved significant ROI with BigCo's products.

To wrap up his credibility presentation, Jack handed Peter the one-page Company Information Sheet (CIS) he and Morena had designed.

Peter quickly read the sheet. "Looks good," he said. "Thanks for the overview."

"You're welcome," said Jack. So far, he'd spent less than two minutes on the call.

Trust-builder #3: Get right down to the meeting's purpose

Jack chuckled to himself as he thought of his first sales call and how much of it he'd squandered on small talk. *Buyer-Approved Sell-*

ing, and his neighbor, were right: During initial meetings, the best way to create trust and rapport was to focus on business.

"That's what a professional visitor does," his neighbor said. "Let friendship come later. Insincere small talk is just a variation on the 'How are you?' approach most reps use.

"Remember, Jack: People buy from people they trust. When you get down to business, and you're helpful and easy to deal with, that's a great start. I didn't ask reps in to talk about the pictures on my desk!"

Trust-builder #4: Ask good questions and take notes

It was true: Good questions got you good answers. Jack listened attentively as Peter gave an informative two-minute reply to his first question.

As Peter spoke, Jack wrote Peter's key points in his meeting planner's note section. He smiled a bit as he recalled his BigCo training. They'd spent four days discussing what reps could *say* to prospects—and completely bypassed the crucial role of listening. And what better way to get listening opportunities than to ask good questions?

Jack's neighbor had put it well: "When you listen, you do more than give your prospect a chance to speak. You show the prospect that you're really interested in their needs, that you're not just trying to 'sell' them. Communication is a two-way street—and that means listening is an essential skill."

The question Peter was answering was one that Jack and Morena had read in *Buyer-Approved Selling.* After modifying it slightly, they agreed it was a great opener for the "prospect interview" stage of the sales call.

Jack's first objective was to quickly determine if Peter's company was a potential BigCo customer. This required Jack to learn six things:

1. What the prospect was doing, or was going to do, as it related to BigCo's products and services
2. Which suppliers they'd been using, or if they were looking for new suppliers
3. When their buying cycle was
4. Where they used a similar product or service
5. Why they needed this type of product or service
6. How BigCo's products and services might be better-suited to the prospect's needs—and if they were, how the prospect's company made their buying decisions

That was exactly what Jack's prepared questions were designed to tell him.

It was Morena's idea to organize their questions this way. "What, Who, When, Where, Why, and How" was a proven formula journalists used to make sure they didn't miss any important information for their stories.

Jack had already answered some of the questions during his research. He used some of that information to form his other questions. Not only was it a good way to get more information about his prospect, but it let the prospect know that Jack had done some research on his company.

Trust-builder #5: Prepare responses to tough questions prospects could ask

Buyer-Approved Selling said that in first meetings, buyers often asked, "Why is your [company, product, service] better than your competitor's?"

"Really, Jack," Morena had said, "if a rep has to stop and think of why her company is better, can it really *be* that much better?"

So they decided to prepare an answer to that key question. They asked their sales managers and some of the reps how they answered it, and were not surprised when they got four very different responses. They created a standard answer using the best content from them.

Sure enough, Peter was now asking Jack that very question—and he was prepared. He promptly and sincerely gave Peter the answer he'd rehearsed. Then he paused for a moment to reflect on how well his call was going, and how powerful he felt by being so well-prepared.

Trust-builder #6: Honor your promises

When Jack proposed their meeting, he'd asked Peter for only 10 minutes of his time. This showed respect for Peter's schedule, and made it more likely Peter would be able to fit him in. Jack now saw that his time was nearly up. "I promised you a structured 10-minute meeting, and our time has run out," he said. "How would you like to proceed?"

"I am especially busy today," Peter replied, "but we can take another 10 or 15 minutes. Or we can reschedule, if you need to get going."

"I'm okay," said Jack. "Thanks for the extra time." Judging from Peter's answers to his questions, it seemed as though their companies could be a good fit.

Jack glanced at his meeting planner. In this next stage of his call, he would make a GPOS (Genuine Preemptive Objection Statement).

The objection-killer

While calling their customer base, Jack and Morena had identified their prospects' top three objections. The most common one was price. BigCo used top-of-the-line materials and spared no expense when it came to quality. As a result, their prices were often considerably higher than their competitors'.

Jack and Morena had put a lot of time into developing their "price" GPOS. How would it go over with Peter?

"As you may know, Peter, our solution's initial price is higher than our competitor's. But due to increased uptime and enhanced durability, the cost of using our product over its average five-year lifespan is 20% *lower* than the industry norm. We'd rather create a better product, and charge a bit more, so we can give you more value and save you the trouble of early replacement."

Peter nodded thoughtfully. "You're right, Jack. I'd heard that BigCo was the industry's most expensive player, and frankly, I was curious why. Your explanation makes sense. Keep going—you haven't scared me off yet!"

The meeting continues

Jack smiled. He and Peter hadn't spent one second on small talk, and there was definite rapport. It was true: The best service you could do for people was to make it clear, quickly and professionally, how you could help them. Jack made a mental note to buy his next-door mentor a bottle of single-malt Scotch. That advice alone had earned it.

"As you know," said Peter, "we're exploring the possibility of moving ahead with a new system, and we've looked at a few vendors. What I haven't told you is that we're in the process of acquiring another company. This information isn't out on the streets yet, but it will be by next week. I feel I can trust you to keep this quiet until we announce it next Monday. This means that whoever we go with will be selling us five systems—three for our location, and two for the new acquisition.

"I'll be asking all the vendors for an analysis of our projected service and maintenance costs. I'll give you Jay Beardsley's number—he's our Operations guy. He'll give you the information you'll need to get a report to me. I'll also need a proposal with leasing terms of 36 and 48 months. It'd be great if I could have all that by the end of next week."

Leave your prospect with some objective questions that could be critical to the purchasing decision

It was time to wrap up the meeting, and again, Jack was prepared: He had two questions to leave with his prospect. "Peter, I've put together a couple of questions that may be helpful to you as you work your way toward a decision. They're fair, objective questions that you may want to ask any vendor you speak to. May I leave them with you?"

Peter took the sheet from Jack and read it. "Interesting . . . I agree, these are good things to consider. Thanks Jack, this is helpful."

Wrapping it up

The meeting was nearly over. There was one more thing to do. "Peter, I just want to recap the key points of our meeting to make sure I'm not missing anything. Is that okay?"

"Fire away, Jack."

"I'm going to call Jay Beardsley in Operations to get the information we need to prepare an analysis of your projected operating and maintenance costs. I'll also prepare a proposal with leasing terms of 36 and 48 months. You mentioned that you needed the proposal by next Friday. How about the operating and maintenance analysis—would you like that Friday as well?"

"Glad you asked. I'll need that by next Wednesday if possible. I'm meeting with Jay on Thursday morning to go over the vendors' reports, and we need them in advance of the proposals."

"No problem," said Jack. "Does that cover everything?"

"There is one more thing. I have a colleague from our industry, and he's also looking at systems. He needs only one, but I'll give you his number. Tell him I sent you, and I'm sure he'll meet with you. I wouldn't normally do this after only one meeting with a sales person—but I have to say Jack, you've impressed me with your professional approach, and I like to refer quality people to my network. They do the same for me."

"Thanks very much, Peter."

"Jack, do you know you're probably only the fifth rep I've met with in the last five years who has handled a call like you did? You sent a meeting agenda ahead of time; you clearly researched our company; and you summarized the call so we could be clear on it. It's not rocket science, but it's important stuff—and I appreciate it."

"And I appreciate your time, and the referral," said Jack with a smile.

Feeling empowered

As Jack drove away from Peter's office, he remembered what his neighbor said about the ideas in *Buyer-Approved Selling*. He'd said they were designed to build trust over time. Jack considered how his Advance Meeting Agenda, and each subsequent step in his meeting plan, had helped him do that. He felt even more confident than before, empowered by his second sales-call experience. He was definitely looking forward to more.

Jack and Morena met for lunch at the sandwich shop next to BigCo. "Wow, Jack—it sounds like your call went awesomely!"

"It was amazing. My second-ever sales meeting, and I can't imagine it going much better. It felt seamless, cohesive . . . I was on a plan from the moment I walked in till the moment I left—and it worked flawlessly. Compared to my first sales call, it was night and day. But tell me more about your call, Morena."

"I got stuck in traffic, so I had lots of time to listen to my taped rehearsal, too. The lady I met with read my email summary before the meeting, and she thanked me for it. I quickly realized that they didn't qualify as a customer. The questions we prepared helped me do that. But I know it's just a matter of time till I find a prospect I can advance to the proposal stage. I feel confident. As far as I'm concerned, our planning paid off for me, too."

"You know what, Morena? We're going to show these BigCo reps who the real shooters are. Give us a year and we'll be where we want to be. I'm incredibly motivated—how about you?"

"Watch me go! But speaking of going, you'd better get back to the office and send your email summary. You've done everything right so far. You can't stop now!"

Trust-builder #7: When appropriate, email a summary of key points and action items discussed on a phone call or in a sales meeting

Jack returned to the office and emailed Peter a summary of the key points from their meeting, as *Buyer-Approved Selling* recommended. He remembered what one of the senior buyers said in the book's research: An email summary was helpful, and gave her a good impression of the rep—yet only 2% of reps she'd dealt with had sent summaries.

Jack smiled. It was the kind of smile you made when you knew something other people didn't. Information was power—but having it and using it were two different things.

Chapter 6
A Whale of an Opportunity

★

There was huge revenue potential. MajorAccountCo had been a BigCo customer until repeated service problems and an aggressive competitor caused them to switch suppliers.

Jack picked up his phone and dialed MajorAccountCo for the fifth time that week. Each time, he'd reached Erik's voice mail. He'd never left a message; his goal was to catch Erik live. The problem was, Erik never seemed to be available.

But Jack was persistent, and he finally got through. After a very brief exchange, Erik less-than-enthusiastically agreed to see Jack.

"Only for 10 or 15 minutes," said Erik, "and I want it to be clear that I will be in charge of the agenda."

"That's fine with me, Erik. I won't waste your time."

"Tell me—how long have you been with BigCo?"

"Less than a month."

Erik laughed. "I'm not surprised. I met with your predecessor five months ago, and I didn't think he'd make it through the meeting."

Jack had done his best to prepare. He did some research on MajorAccountCo, read reports from his company's customer service logs, and spoke with Mark, his customer service manager.

"Three reps have had your territory in the past three-and-a-half years," Mark told him. "They've all met with Erik, to no avail. He's a seriously tough cookie, with no love in his heart for BigCo. He's probably heard that we're introducing our new GH749A System next quarter, and he's meeting with you just to keep up on industry news. It's too bad they had that recurring problem with our system—the downtime cost them a lot. We made some mistakes."

So Jack had good reasons to feel uncertain as he drove to his appointment with Erik the next week. He planned to be honest with Erik about BigCo's mistakes, to validate his feelings of resentment, and to show him how things could be different.

With no control over the agenda, there was no need to send Erik an Advance Meeting Agenda. That felt wrong to Jack, like a basic part of the process was missing. But how many reps would care about that in any case?

He pulled into a visitor spot at MajorAccountCo and walked briskly towards the main entrance. "A businessperson might consider walking a bit faster than average," Jack's neighbor told him. "Not so you look like you're running late, but so you look like someone with a purpose."

As he waited in MajorAccountCo's ornate marble lobby, Jack felt a rush of adrenaline, as he'd felt sometimes when playing hockey. He never thought business could feel so competitive. It certainly did, though, in this world of commission-based sales—especially with big stakes like MajorAccountCo. If he succeeded in recapturing MajorAccountCo's business, he would not only be a hero at work, he would earn a staggering commission. The sale would fill 10 months of his quota.

Jack meets Erik

As he entered Erik Brandt's office, Jack could tell that things weren't exactly warm and fuzzy. As soon as they sat down, Erik said,

"I agreed to meet with you as long as it was on my terms. I don't mind telling you that I'm just after information—and I think I'm entitled to it, considering the business we've done with your company. That's the only reason I agree to see you BigCo reps. So there's no point hoping for a sale anytime soon."

Introducing Erik to *Buyer-Approved Selling*

Jack had no planned response to what Erik said, but as he listened, he had an idea. He opened his leather case and found his copy of *Buyer-Approved Selling*. It was worn and dog-eared—and it was perfect.

Jack leaned forward with the book in his hands. "Erik, I want you to know I appreciate and understand where you're coming from. I read our customer service logs and I met with our customer service manager. We cost you money, and it was our fault that we lost your business."

Jack paused for a few seconds to let this sink in. Then he leaned back in his chair, looked up at Erik with a determined expression.

"Erik, I would like the chance to have a serious meeting with you to objectively explore if we're the company that can provide the best solution for you. Last year our new level-three systems helped XyzCo to reduce overhead by 17%. That's been verified."

Jack held up the book. "If you agree to meet with me and give us a second chance, you should know that I'll be following a new communication-based sales system that's described in this book I'm holding. It's called *Buyer-Approved Selling: Sales Secrets from the Buyer's Side of the Desk.* Over two hundred buyers were interviewed for it, and the foreword was written by Christopher Locke, the global lead buyer at DaimlerChrysler."

Jack handed the book to him, and Erik glanced through it. "Hmm, this is interesting. I've never heard of a sales system endorsed by buyers. Now, here's a good chapter: 'How to Annoy

Buyers, Guaranteed.' There's a good chapter for a sales book." He continued to flip through it. "'Send an email summary of key points from a meeting.' You know, only a couple of reps I deal with do that. How did they research this book?"

Jack showed him the section that explained the book's research process. "Really," Erik said. "They asked over 4300 questions—sounds like a well-researched book. Do you find it helpful?"

"Amazingly so," said Jack. "I've been using all the tips consistently. They require a lot of planning, preparation, and rehearsal, but it's worth it. I did the first sales call of my life a few weeks ago, using this information, and it went flawlessly. That meeting may produce my first sale. I should find out tomorrow."

"Well, I must say, it does seem like an obvious way to sell—but no one has ever organized the information like this."

"Erik, why don't you let me demonstrate the book's Buyer-Approved approaches first-hand? I'm confident you'd find it a refreshing experience. Can we start on those terms?"

"Okay, I'm curious enough," Erik said, without a trace of a smile. He flipped through his schedule. "I can meet with you the last Thursday of next month, the 28th. I'll give you 45 minutes. Well, I need to get going, I'm running late. See you on the 28th."

The next day, Jack received an email from Erik asking where he could get a copy of the book. Jack emailed him the toll-free number from the book's last page.

Post-meeting discussion

"Elation," Jack said to Morena over a black cup of Sumatra coffee. "That's what I felt when he penciled me in for an appointment. I'm excited, Morena. I really think I have a shot at this deal.

"Erik is a serious, no-nonsense kind of guy—but under all that, I think he's fair. I'd bet on it. He's a guy with principles who likes a quid-pro-quo business relationship, an equal exchange. We dropped the ball with him, but now we're getting a second chance. He knows I'll be using a selling system based on feedback from his colleagues, and he knows I'm a brand-new rep. What do I have to lose?"

"What did your team say when you told them?" Morena asked.

"No one at the office thinks I have a chance," Jack scowled. "They think it was a fluke. Of course I didn't tell them about *Buyer-Approved Selling,* and how it influenced the call. They'll have to wait until we've proven this system works—and if we do, we may see the whole sales team using it."

"I like how you leveraged the book in the call, Jack. A buyer would be curious about it. What a great ice-breaker!"

"No doubt," Jack replied. "It turned the call around. Putting the whole sales perspective where it belongs, on the buyer's side—that intrigued him."

The first sale

"It reminds me of my first touchdown with the regional league," Jack said, as Bart listened with a smile. "It's just as exciting."

Bart looked at Jack for a moment. "I have to say, your enthusiasm is infectious. It's good to see some of that around here. Keep up the good work, and congratulations."

Jack called Morena's extension and told her the good news. "Cool, isn't it? My very first sales call leads to my first sale."

"That's terrific, Jack!"

"Peter said he may have another referral for me, too. He wants to wait till our system is up and running for a few weeks; then he'll pass it along. How's it going at your end?"

Down to the wire

"I followed up with a prospect this morning. They said it was down to the wire between us and CompeteCo. They'll make their decision by the end of next week. It's frustrating, though. I hate having to sit around, with no way to influence the decision. Sure, a 50/50 chance is good—but there's no second place in sales. There must be something I can do without being annoying. Any ideas?"

"How about sending your buyer a copy of the book? It's not like giving out golf passes or NBA tickets. It's clearly a business tool, and I bet it would be well-received. You could include a handwritten note explaining that you follow the book's system, and that you wanted her to know in advance what she could expect from you if she decided to go with us."

"Great idea, Jack! There's nothing to lose, and everything to gain. It's proactive, and all business. I'll get an extra copy and send it right away."

The solution, or the problem?

The next day didn't start out with congratulations and happy vibes.

Five minutes after Jack walked into the office, the phone on his desk rang with the distinctive sound that meant an outside call. He answered promptly, thinking it might be a prospect calling to place an order.

It wasn't. The voice on the phone belonged to an existing customer—and she was mad.

"BigCo made another mistake on my billing. That's the fourth month in a row! This is #*&@! unacceptable!" Jack winced at the unexpected profanity.

Jack knew how the guys on the team would handle this. He'd heard them do it. He could tell Jenny that he was late for a meeting and that he'd have customer service call her right back.

But he didn't. Instead, he heard himself say, "You have every right to be annoyed, Jenny. You're right, it's completely unacceptable. That's not working for you—and it's not working for me, not on my shift. Are you going to be in your office in the next hour? I'd like to come right over and straighten this out for you personally. I can go over your account with our billing department before I leave, and we can settle this once and for all for you."

"Uh—well, sure. Okay." Suddenly Jenny didn't sound nearly as mad.

Five minutes later, Jack was in the billing department going over Jenny's billing. The Accounts Receivable clerk was a helpful young woman named Masako. "Thanks very much for stepping in and helping with this problem," she said. "It's not your fault, so I really appreciate your time."

"It's no problem at all. A wise friend told me that we had a choice in life: We can be part of the problem, or part of the solution."

"Well, you're the only sales rep I know that's ever taken this kind of initiative. If there's anything my department can do for one of your customers, just call me and I'll put it in action."

"Thanks, Masako." With Jenny's billing in hand, he drove off to see if he could solve Jenny's problem. He was starting to realize that sales was not only about selling; it was also about keeping things sold.

Bad news is a fast traveler

It was a 20-minute drive to Jenny's office. Jack remembered a conversation with Morena, when they were discussing the idea of exceeding customer expectations. Morena told him about a study she'd read that showed some startling facts:

- A really unsatisfied customer tells everyone they know about their problem, even after they have quit being your customer.
- Customers who had a serious problem corrected quickly and competently became the most loyal customers.

- Unless you communicate openly, honestly, and regularly with your customers, you run a major risk of losing them.

Face to face with Jenny

"You got here quickly," Jenny said, offering Jack a seat in her office. "The way BigCo has been treating us lately, I didn't think you'd be so prompt. Many big companies seem to have lost the human touch these days. We have only 35 employees, and we're all about the personal touch. So maybe you can understand why it rubs me the wrong way when I get treated like a number."

Jack leaned forward in his chair to make it clear he was giving Jenny his full attention. "What exactly are the problems you're having with BigCo?"

"Well, I've already told you about the erroneous billings. I've faxed them back each time, but no replies. So I've had to get on the phone and explain them all over again."

Jack asked Jenny which fax number she was using. "This one." She handed him the business card of the BigCo rep who'd filled their original order.

Jack saw the problem right away: That fax machine was in the sales department. He'd seen how easily faxes got lost or discarded when they didn't relate directly to sales.

By the end of their meeting, Jenny was smiling. "I'm sorry for cussing you out, but it takes me 40 minutes to try to balance my figures against your statement. This was the fourth time, and I just lost it—and you were the poor guy on the other end of my wrath."

"Don't worry about it, Jenny. I'm just glad we could get it sorted out so it wouldn't happen again."

"Keep up the good work, Jack. And keep taking care of our account. We may be small, but we're in a big industry, and I'm on the board of directors for our industry association chapter. I know people."

Jack left Jenny's office thinking how well-spent the time had been. He was working to develop a positive reputation in his industry—and pleasing someone like Jenny was a good way to do it.

Chapter 7
Doing the Right Thing

★

"**As much as I love cold calling,**" Morena laughed, "there's no way I'd do it every day if I didn't have a way to make myself do it. And the only way I know how to do that is with a schedule."

"You're right. With all this planning and preparation, I've let too many cold-call days get by me, too. We're already into our second month. Let's get a cold-call routine going."

They agreed to start coming to work at 8 A.M. so they could make an hour of prospecting calls each day. It took some getting used to. Neither of them were particularly early risers. Before long, though, it felt like a normal part of their day.

They also found it much easier to reach decision-makers early in the morning, because:

- Many busy executives began their days early to get in extra work time.
- The execs were generally more receptive to calls before they became tied up with the day's business.
- Many execs' receptionists and assistants didn't arrive till 9:00, so they often answered their own phones before then.

Jack and Morena also scheduled an hour of prospecting every afternoon from 3:30 to 4:30. That kept them off the road during rush hour, which helped keep stress low and performance high. They found it surprisingly easy to direct prospects to specific appointment times, allowing them to avoid further traffic.

They examined the stats from their previous calls. They determined that, each hour, they could make an average of 18.5 calls and connect with three decision-makers. That added up to ten hours a week of prospecting calls, yielding an average of 30 decision-maker conversations each week. This new schedule helped each of them generate an average of ten qualified appointments every week. That was in addition to the call-in leads, which generated an average of five appointments per week.

Between their prospecting calls and the company's marketing efforts, Jack and Morena were doing an average of three appointments a day, which they usually scheduled at 9:30, 11:00, and 1:30. None of their appointments was more than a 30-minute drive in any given territory, especially during non-rush-hour periods. It worked out to a very efficient use of their time.

"Wow," said Morena. "It's amazing how many appointments we're managing to generate, with a little planning and a routine!"

Closing the sale is not complicated

"People sure like to make things complicated," said Jack, showing Morena the large sales section at Humongous Bookstore. "Check this out: *31 Ways to Close a Sale.* That's one closing method for each day of the month! What a contrast to *Buyer-Approved Selling.*"

When Jack made his first sale, he'd done what *Buyer-Approved Selling* recommended: He kept it simple. "Peter, we can have your system up and running for the first of the month, no problem. Is there anything else you need to know to move ahead with this order?"

Peter had replied, "No, I think I know all I need to know. Let's get it going."

No tricks, no complicated techniques, no pressure. Jack had shown Peter *why* he should do business with BigCo. When you did that, you didn't have to use tricky closes; the deal practically closed itself.

"I just thought of a good analogy for closing the sale, Morena. It's like an iceberg. The base represents the huge amount of work that led you to the close. The tip represents the one simple question which is the close. As long as you ensure that your question is not manipulative or pushy, and that it focuses on the buyer's interests, you're good to go."

"That's good, Jack. Hey, you could call it the Iceberg Close."

"Yes, and we could use it any day of the month!"

Do it well, teach it well: Two steps to mastering the art of anything

"Once our careers are really in gear, Jack, I think you should consider teaching sales," Morena said, "You're out to master sales, and they say that to master something, you must be able to teach it, too."

"They also say, 'Those who can, do—and those who can't, teach'!" Jack laughed.

"Okay, but my brother swears that the 'killer combo' is mastering both the arts of doing and teaching. He started teaching in his field by the end of his first year. He learned all he could—he really went crazy with it—so he could be an expert in his field. Now he gets $7,000 for a one-hour speaking engagement."

Teaching. Jack thought about it later that night. It always seemed that it would be fun to teach part-time, and it made sense to teach people what you did every day. It would keep him accountable, too: When you presume to show people how to do something, you had to "walk your talk." And it would help Jack position himself as an expert in his industry.

A fear worse than death?

"Teaching—that's interesting," said Jack's neighbor. "Did you know that many people rate public speaking—standing alone in front of a room full of people—as their number-one fear, right up there with dying?"

"No way. You're kidding!" said Jack.

"It's true. Surveys have shown it. So, how are your public speaking skills, Jack? Have you done much of it?"

"I've spoken to large groups only twice, at weddings. I've never spoken in a business setting. I need to learn more about it. What do you recommend?"

"There's the Dale Carnegie public speaking course, and there's Toastmasters. They both offer businesspeople a way to practice and develop speaking skills. It's a vital skill for accelerating your career. I read a quote from Charles M. Schwab, who was one of the wealthiest men in America. He said, 'I'll pay more for a man's ability to speak and express himself than for any other quality he might possess.' That always stuck with me. I studied and mastered the art of public speaking, and it did wonders for my career. When you present yourself well on stage, it can raise people's perceptions of you higher than your actual experience. How can you complain about that?"

"I'm convinced," said Jack. "I'm going to become a public-speaking expert. I'll ask Morena if she'd like to sign up for a course with me."

Thanks, but no thanks

"Absolutely no way!" cried Morena when Jack raised the topic. "I have no doubt you'll be a good speaker, Jack. But there's no way you'll get me in front of a large group. I'm fine with a few people. Job interviews, sales meetings, presentations—no problem. But I had to speak in front of my university class once, and it was horrible. My mouth dried up, my throat got tight, my heart pounded, and I started sweating like crazy. I think my teeth were chattering, too. Don't laugh, Jack—I'm not kidding!"

"I'm not laughing at you. But you know what they say: To conquer fear, you must do what you fear most."

"Normally, I'd agree with you, Jack. But in this case—sorry, I have no desire to conquer this particular fear. It's just not for me. Maybe you think I'd be a good speaker because I like to chat so much. I'm not like that in front of a group. As soon as I get up there, I lose it."

So Jack registered alone for a series of four-hour weekly classes. He could already tell that he was going to miss Morena's contagious energy.

60 sales calls a month! The schedule is working

It was their third month at BigCo and Jack and Morena were working their schedule consistently. They'd maintained their average of three appointments a day, 60 appointments a month. Compared to their fellow sales reps, that put them at the top of the curve.

This achievement didn't come without a price. Jack's and Morena's lives were considerably different now. TV and mid-week nights out with friends were things of the past. They were replaced by research, planning and rehearsing for sales calls, and developing proposals—and, in Jack's case, attending speaking classes.

Sales kickoff

"Our new systems are coming out on Friday," Jack told his neighbor as he poured him a cold beer in a frosted mug. "And we're having a sales kickoff to officially introduce them."

"Must be nice to be selling new gear in your fourth month on the job, Jack. Do these new systems offer any advantages that could help you with the MajorAccountCo deal?"

"I hope. We don't get the final specs till the kickoff, but if the rumors are true, the new GH749A's low operating costs will blow our competition out of the water. I want that deal so bad I can taste it."

The new systems arrive

"Congratulations to everyone in the sales division," announced BigCo's president, James Farrell, as he spoke to the 73 sales reps, their managers, the four-member sales support team, and the VP of sales. "You can all stand a little taller today. With the release of the GH749A System, we are the new industry leader. Team, the rumors are true: The GH749A costs 17% less to operate than its closest rival."

The sales team clapped and whistled. After sharing more details—with appropriate fanfare—James concluded: "The GH749A has set a new standard for our industry. So get out there and make sure everyone knows about it. Good luck, and good selling!"

MajorAccountCo revisited

Less is more, Jack thought, as he finished his new Company Information Sheet. He was preparing for his appointment with Erik at MajorAccountCo. Erik had rescheduled the meeting six weeks later than the original date, but it worked out perfectly: Jack could now tell him about the new GH749A.

The appointment was only three days away, and Jack was excited about taking Erik through the *Buyer-Approved Selling* system. He focused on the Advance Meeting Agenda (AMA) he would email Erik before their meeting.

MajorAccountCo meeting summary

"Okay, out with it buddy," Morena said. "How did it go at MajorAccountCo yesterday?"

They were sitting outside Morena's favorite coffee shop, where they often met before work. Morena always ordered esoteric concoctions like "Grande Non-Fat Double-Shot Americano with Just a Sprinkle of Cinnamon."

Jack, on the other hand, was content with plain black coffee. The shop's beans were always burned, and the coffee seemed especially high in caffeine. That worked for him.

"All right," laughed Jack. "It's only 7:20 A.M., though—give a guy a chance to wake up! First, tell me what happened with the woman you sent a copy of *Buyer-Approved Selling*. That was a while ago, and I've had no updates."

"Oops, I should have told you, especially since that was your idea. Two weeks after I sent her the book, she called and thanked me for it. She'd been busy, but she finally got a chance to look at it, and she was impressed. She even knew one of the buyers quoted in the book—they belonged to the same chapter of a national buyers' association. She said, 'I'm putting you on our short list. If you're using this book, we should get along fine.' It's a four-system deal, Jack. They should have an answer by the end of next week."

"Way to go, Morena! Not only has the book taught us a lot about selling, it's become a bridge to some of our buyers."

"Okay, Jack, you look awake now. Your turn—MajorAccountCo."

"Well, I covered all the bases on planning and preparation. I rehearsed the call with my neighbor. I felt great about my prospects—but even that didn't prepare me for what happened. To use one of our sales team's buzzwords, the meeting went 'seamlessly'. Erik's adversarial style melted away. I felt like I was meeting with a different person.

"When I summarized the key points at the end of the meeting and asked Erik if there was anything else, he said, 'Only one thing. I want to apologize for how I treated you. I had a grudge against BigCo, and I shouldn't have taken it out on you. You put a lot of work and professionalism into this meeting, and I appreciate it.'

"That made my day. They won't be doing anything until their fiscal year-end, and that's three months away—so it's not time to celebrate yet. But I feel good about my chances. Well, we'd better go hit the phones. It's getting late—it's already 7:45 A.M.!"

Time Out: A Word from Jack

Hello, Reader, this is Jack. Do you have a quick minute?

When I was asked to be in this book, I hesitated. But the more I thought about it, the more I realized I couldn't say no. There's too much good stuff in my story not to pass it along. I hope you're picking up some ideas that you can use to be more successful in your work.

At this point, you may be wondering: *How can this guy work like such a dog, and have no life?*

I'll tell you why: Because I'm looking at this as an investment in a *better* life. It's the same as when I was in university full-time, with two part-time jobs. I had "no life" then, either. That was an investment in my future, too—and now I'm living that future. I'm glad I made sacrifices and delayed gratification to earn my degree. I wouldn't change that for anything.

You see, I'm determined to be in the top 20% of my company's reps—or higher. I also want to win Sales Rep of the Month a few times a year and get that parking spot. If I achieve those goals, I'll earn *three times* what the average rep earns. That's important to me, because I don't consider myself average. And neither should you.

If you want to make your goals a reality, you have to be sure you pick the right goals. You need to find goals that make you passionate—goals that get you out of bed early and keep you up late. For me, they are earning a nice six-figure income, and being considered an expert at what I do.

I'm also working extra-hard because it's not my style to be unprepared, to "wing it." Preparation pays for itself—not just in sales, but in how you feel about yourself, and about what you do.

The way I see it, if you're going to commit to a new job, it needs to be for at least a year, and you have to give it everything you've got. Otherwise, how will you ever know how well you could have done?

As sales people, we're typically given a lot of discretion with our time. If you don't use that freedom wisely, it can be a big *dis*advantage. Some of my teammates are great golfers, and they play only during the week, when the courses aren't as busy. You get my drift.

When you've decided to invest in your future, your work is your life and your life is your work—at least for a while. Your life includes:

- Getting up on time
- Shopping for work attire (and working to pay for it)
- Paying attention to exercise and nutrition, to stay sharp
- Traveling to and from work
- Taking work home

Seem overwhelming? It can. But if I'm going to go to work every day, I'm going to make as much money as I can so my loved ones will have a better life.

I also try to remember that **80/20 is the way to go.** In the sales world, 20% of the reps make 80% of the commissions. They don't get there by accident or luck. They get there by spending their time on the 20% of activities that return 80% of the results they seek.

I'm prepared to give 12 months of extra effort to have a shot at the Top 20 Percent Club. As any sales manager will tell you: Work it hard in Year One—real hard—and you will love Year Two and Year Three.

My neighbor says that if I keep up the quality work in Year Two and beyond, I can start to reduce the amount of time I put in. As I gain experience, develop relationships with my buyers, and develop my network and my reputation, my 60-65 hour weeks should go down to 40-45. I can live with that. Meanwhile, I'm applying the 80/20 Rule to prioritize my activities and to keep my life balanced.

Well, thanks for the time-out. I wanted you to understand: I may be working like a madman, but I'm not crazy.

Sincerely, **JACK**

P.S.: Keep reading. Things start to get real interesting.

Chapter 8
Network Connections

★

"**Congratulations to both of us!**" said Morena, clinking her glass against Jack's. It was Friday evening, just after work, and they were out for an overdue celebratory drink. "We made it through the 90-day Probation Hoop. And here we are, going on four months!"

"Seems a lot longer, doesn't it? So much has happened. I'll tell you, though, when it comes to product knowledge and overall selling ability, I already feel on par with some of the old pros on my team. How about you?"

"You know, Jack, I believe I do. But think of all those hours we spent role-playing those system demos. There's only so much you can learn about a GH350, or even a GS700. It isn't rocket science, relating our systems features and benefits to the buyers' needs."

"Well, Morena, here's to you for keeping us on track, being sure we worked like dogs all those weeknights and weekends. Especially in our first month—man, that was tough!"

"It was worth it, though, Jack. It took some brainpower and lots of hours. But look at the predictable selling system we've created with the help of *Buyer-Approved Selling*. We both did over 70% of quota in our second and third months! My manager says that most new reps do only 50%. He was pleased when I came in at 76."

"That's right—you beat me by 4%, too. But my manager was impressed with my 72%. When he gave our VP his original forecast, he had me at 50—so as far as he's concerned, I'm 22% over quota!"

"I still think it's pretty cool that you and I had the most active proposals on our teams last month. Too bad they don't give bonuses for that."

Networking and connecting

Morena bumped into Jack the next week in the lunchroom. "Do you want to go to a Board of Trade event at the Four Seasons, after work on Thursday? There'll be over 800 people, with a buffet and a bar. It's a combination mini-tradeshow and business networking session."

"I'm in," replied Jack. "My neighbor was just saying that we should join our local chamber of commerce. The Board of Trade is essentially a chamber of commerce for downtown. They hold all the big events. BigCo will pay for our memberships, too.

"Have you ever been to a networking event, Jack? I haven't."

"Me neither. Sounds like fun, though. Who knows, we could make some good contacts. You know the saying: 'It's not what you know, it's who you know'? My neighbor says, 'It's not who you know—it's who knows you.'"

"I'm just glad your neighbor knew *you*, or we wouldn't have gotten hold of *Buyer-Approved Selling*!"

The Frog and Prince

Jack and Morena invited Jack's neighbor and his wife, Barb, to a backyard barbecue.

"Effective business networking isn't just a matter of showing up, shaking a few hands, and exchanging a few business cards," Jack's neighbor was saying, as they sat at the picnic table in Jack's backyard. "It's like anything: You can do it well or poorly, and the results speak for themselves."

Jack wanted to give his neighbor his full attention, but he had to keep an eye on the salmon he was cooking. With Jack's "famous" West Coast BBQ sauce, the fresh Pacific salmon was a sure winner.

Then Jack's neighbor said something Jack couldn't miss.

"How would you and Morena like to learn networking from the man who has been the managing director of the Board of Trade for the past 20 years?"

Two heads nodded.

"It so happens I know him personally. I was on a business trip years ago, and he was working at the company I was visiting. He's a good friend now, and he sent me a copy of his new bestseller, *The Frog and Prince: Secrets of Positive Networking.* I just finished it, and I assure you, it will teach you everything you need to know for when you go to the Board of Trade's 'Business after Business' event. I'll lend it to you, but I'll need it back. It's a signed copy."

A toast to mentorship

That night after dinner, Jack stood up and tapped his glass as if he were at a large banquet. He looked at Morena, then Barb, and finally, his neighbor. "To my friend, neighbor, and business mentor: This toast is to all the experiences that have allowed you to accumulate the wisdom and knowledge you share with us so freely. What a tremendous difference it's made. Here's to you!"

Networking for business:
It's not who you know, it's who knows you

The next week, Morena was saying goodbye to Jack at the end of the Board of Trade event. "Jack, that networking book was an excellent resource. I used five tips from it tonight—stuff I wouldn't have thought to do on my own. Chalk up one more for your neighbor. He really does come through for us."

"That was a great event. We made some awesome contacts—the kind of people you *want* to know.'"

Stay in touch by giving extra value

Jack had been wondering how to use a particular tip in *Buyer-Approved Selling:* "Stay in touch with your customers by providing them with useful information and resources."

"There's a fine line between annoying people and keeping in touch with them," Jack's neighbor had told him. What kinds of "useful information and resources" could Jack provide?

The answer practically walked into him at a Board of Trade networking event, when he met the editor of a new trade publication specific to MajorAccountCo's industry. The editor gave Jack the debut issue, and another to pass along to Erik, with an extra business card.

That was as serendipitous as it got! Erik liked to keep up with industry news, and the editor could be a good contact for him, too. He'd probably end up subscribing to the magazine—the magazine he got from Jack.

The MajorAccountCo touch-point pays off

"How's it going with MajorAccountCo?" asked Bart, while they were going over Jack's accounts. "Any contact with Erik?"

"As you know, they're not making any decisions till they get ready for their new fiscal year. But I just had an interesting chance for a touch-point with Erik, and it was nothing annoying or pushy." He told Bart about meeting the trade-magazine editor, and how he'd left the debut issue for Erik at MajorAccountCo's reception.

An announcement came over the paging system: "Jack Fontaine, call on extension 2472."

"Here, use my phone—maybe it's Erik." He dialed the extension and handed the phone to Jack.

Jack hung up a few minutes later. "How did you know?" he asked. "He was calling to thank me for the magazine and the editor's card. He's going to call the editor to see if he can get one of his industry articles published."

"I heard you ask Erik if you could meet with one of their key system users, to help you gather more specific data for the proposal."

"That's right. Now I have their main system operator's name and number. Erik said, 'You're lucky to have the chance to meet the guy. His opinion will carry weight when they make the final decision.' He also said, 'You know, Jack, none of your competing reps asked to meet with a system user.'"

"Good work Jack. I'm impressed. You really have your ducks lined up. I like that about you. What about the financial decision-maker? Any chance you can identify and meet with them as well?"

"I had an idea on that. When I asked Erik if he was going to lease or purchase, he said it would probably be a lease. I asked him if anyone else would be involved in selecting the lease terms—residual value, term, would it be an operating lease, that sort of thing. He told me their VP Finance would be part of it. So I was hoping I could arrange a meeting between our leasing manager and their VP of finance. It might be helpful to them. You have to admit, some of our more creative leasing programs can be confusing, even to a numbers guy."

"Sounds good, Jack. You have a few months yet before their fiscal year, so keep going like you are—one step at a time, with no pressure. I'm beginning to think you may have a real shot at this. Your commission alone would make any of us green with envy, and you'd be a shoe-in for the Hawaii-Mexico trip."

Jenny gives Jack a reward

A few weeks after his conversation with Erik in Bart's office, Jack got another good-news call. It was Jenny, and she sounded like she had something up her sleeve.

"How's your day going so far, Jack?"

"So far so good, Jenny—but my spider sense tells me it may get even better."

"You're right. I told you I was on the board of directors for our local industry association chapter. We had a meeting last night. One of the members is looking for a new system. I told him I'd give you his number and to expect a call from you. Hope you don't mind."

"That's great! Thanks very much for thinking of me. I really appreciate the referral."

"No worries. You deserve it, with all the extra time and attention you give our little company. Now that you're our account rep, we're starting to like BigCo again. We like their system, we like the service—and thanks to you, our billing is right on the money!"

"Thanks, Jenny—that's great to hear."

"You know, Jack, my friends call me Jen for short."

"Okay, Jen. I'm going to call your friend and see if it makes sense for us to meet. I'll let you know how it goes."

Lunch for the top performers

Jack's team was the top revenue-generator for the last quarter. They were out for a celebratory lunch with the VP of sales. Jack watched Herman as he spoke *at* their waiter in a haughty, dismissive tone.

"You can judge someone's character by how they treat the waiter," Jack's neighbor had said. If that was true, it was clear that Herman was hurting in the character department.

Goodbye, Herman

Three weeks later, the news was all over the company: Herman was history.

"Finally!" Morena exclaimed over lunch. "Someone upstairs had some sense. I wonder who let him go? It must've been the president or the executive VP."

"Don't know, don't care!" Jack said with gusto. "I'm so glad to have him the hell out of the way. The guy caused more damage than good. He'd give an aspirin a headache!"

The new, improved VP of Sales

It was only a week before the new VP of sales appeared.

As the sales department gathered in the company auditorium, Jack wondered what the new VP would be like. All he knew was that his name was Brian Stevenson, and that he'd been sales VP for an electronics hardware company in a neighboring state.

From the moment Brian was introduced and began speaking, it was clear that he and Herman couldn't have been more different. For 30 minutes he spoke passionately about putting the customer first, revolutionizing the industry from a sales perspective, and cleaning up the industry's tarnished image. Short-term profits didn't interest him, he said. He described a five-year plan to make BigCo the industry leader in client satisfaction. Once that happened, he said, sales revenue would be where it needed to be.

"We will always think in terms of each customer's lifetime value," he proclaimed. "In a few weeks, you'll get a new set of customer-centric guidelines. We will start treating everyone consistently. That means no more price discretion, where Customer A pays 20-30% more than Customer B. No more stretching the truth to make quota. It's bad for our image, for our reputation, and for our business.

"My role is to focus on two areas: The things we should not do, and the things we *must* do. In the spirit of my mandate—to focus on the long term—we'll provide you sales reps with new financial incentives that focus on achieving your annual quota, as opposed to your monthly quotas. We are going to think BIG PICTURE!"

Later that week, Brian visited each sales team and spent several minutes speaking with each sales rep.

"I like him," said Morena as she and Jack sipped their morning coffees. "He's real. He listens to people. What a difference from the dictator we had till now."

"I agree," said Jack. "When we spoke, it was uncanny how he reminded me of my neighbor—how he asked questions and listened so intently. He makes you feel like you're the only person in the room."

The key to success

"Speaking of communicating, Jack, are you still taping your calls and reviewing them? My recorder broke, so I haven't been taping for the last week or so."

"I can lend you mine a few times a week till you get a new one. And yes, I still record and review my calls. I'm down to taping just twice a week now—Mondays and Thursdays. I still notice improvement from month to month. I always find something to work on."

"Yes—funny, isn't it? But it sure beats being complacent about it. The taping has made a huge difference for me. Last week I played one of the first tapes I ever made, from six months ago. Then I put on my latest one. It was like listening to two different people! Communication is the number one key to success."

"How about communicating from a stage, though, Morena?"

"Zing! Okay, you got me there, Jack. Nope, that's still where I draw the line."

Gotta have backup

It was the middle of his sixth month at BigCo, and Jack was home with the flu.

The phone rang. It was Morena. "Hope you're feeling better. I have some good news to cheer you up. I'm in my car, and I'm leaving a place called Symbazium Molecular. I have a signed order for two GH500's and one GH749A. And listen to this, Jack: It's *your deal!*"

"Whoa—I'm delirious as it is. I never heard of Symbazium Molecular. How can it be my deal?"

"Remember how we took that advice from *Buyer-Approved Selling* and designated each other as backups when we had to be away? Well, Peter called for me when he heard you were away sick, and he gave me a lead for you. Well, not even a lead—he made the sale *for* you, Jack! All I had to do was stop by to take care of the paperwork."

"Wow—I hope I can cover like that for you sometime! Thanks, Morena. I'm feeling better already."

Chapter 9
Leveraging Expertise

★

It was Jack's seventh month at BigCo and MajorAccountCo's new fiscal year was only three months away. He had other things to think about, though, as he continued to generate 60 appointments each month. He'd made quota twice in the last three months, and Morena had made it once. When they had missed, it was by only a small margin. Things were looking good.

MajorAccountCo: An update

Erik liked Jack's idea to arrange a meeting between BigCo's leasing manager and MajorAccountCo's VP of finance. However, Erik wanted to wait until they were closer to their decision time. It had been six weeks since they last spoke, and Jack was trying to think of another way he could give Erik some useful information in order to stay in touch.

"What do you think about asking BigCo to host an informational seminar?" Jack asked Morena as they headed into the office. "That's an idea from *Buyer-Approved Selling*. We could highlight the new technologies we're developing for the next generation of systems."

"A lot of my customers are already asking about the new gear," Morena replied, "even though it won't be available for another year and a half. So I think there would be a lot of interest."

"I need a reason to call MajorAccountCo, and some other accounts. And a seminar would be a great prospecting tool."

Information-based seminars: An effective prospecting tool

That evening, Jack created a proposal to BigCo with an outline of the seminar. He sent Bart a copy, and as a last-minute thought, CC'd it to the new VP of sales as well.

The next afternoon, there was a voice-mail message from Bart, asking him to meet him and Brian, the new sales VP, at 7:30 the next morning.

"Good morning Brian, Bart," said Jack as he walked into Bart's office the next day.

"Have a seat, Jack," said Brian. "I wanted to talk to you and Bart about your email. At my last company, we often held these kinds of seminars, and we did well with them. They were a regular part of our marketing, and helped us maintain our position as an industry leader. So I'm sold on your idea, and Bart's sold. We just need to work out the logistics."

"Great!" Jack replied.

"In your email, you said you'd be willing to speak about the new technologies and how they will enhance our customers' systems. Jack, what qualifies you to speak on this subject? You've been at BigCo only seven months, correct?

"That's right, but I've been researching the new technology and I've become a bit of an expert. Last night I downloaded a ten-page report by Tsumatsa Technologies, who helped design the digital ASGF filter for the new GH749A. That technology will have the most impact on our new systems. The report went into great detail about integrating the new digital modules into existing systems. If I get your OK, I'll call them and see if I can get permission to use their report for the seminar."

"What about your public-speaking experience? That's an important consideration for me."

"I've just finished a 12-week public speaking course, and I'm a member of Toastmasters. I'm very comfortable speaking in front of large groups, so no worries there."

"All right," Brian said, after they'd gone over their ideas for the seminar. "Leave it with me. I'll let you know where we stand by the end of the week."

The seminar is a go

On Friday afternoon, Brian called Jack into his office.

"Jack, I want you to know that I welcome the kind of initiative you've shown me, and I appreciate the time you spent on your seminar plan. I don't believe in an ego-driven hierarchy. I think a company can get some of its best ideas from people on the front lines.

"So I'm glad to tell you that the seminar is a go. We want you to speak on your topic for 20 minutes. Here's the new outline for the seminar. As you can see, I've made some changes—the most exciting one being the new prototype. HQ just told me they're going to lend us one to display. That should help bring 'em in!"

"Terrific. Have you considered a venue? And what kind of timeframe are we looking at?"

"We'll conduct it in our auditorium, eight weeks from now. We'll have printed invitations for you reps to hand out next week."

Touchpoint

When the invitations were ready, Jack called Erik to give him the news.

"Count me in. I'm looking forward to seeing the new prototype, and to hearing you speak."

"Glad you can make it, Erik. See you there."

When Jack hung up, he smiled. It seemed like it was all coming together.

Marshalling internal resources

Jack and Morena were already starting to stand out from their fellow sales reps. They always took the time to show appreciation to the people who supported them—whether it was a lunch invitation, a cup of coffee brought to a desk, or just a friendly greeting ("Hi, Mark, how's your day going?"). Their commitment and thoughtfulness brought them big esteem from their support staff, and they were getting some attention from BigCo's administration.

The extra effort had a reciprocal effect: They could always depend on timely, friendly support for their customers. Many customers commented on the extra attention they'd received.

"We're lucky to have such good allies at BigCo," Jack told Morena. "Customer Service bent over backwards to help me get that ABeeCeeCo deal."

"Yes, Jack, but remember the last time they went out of their way to help you? You took them all out for lunch. They remembered that. How many of the other reps do that kind of thing?"

The best policy

It was mid-afternoon, and Jack was returning from a meeting. "Hey Jack, wait up!" Morena shouted from across the parking lot.

"I just sold four GH749A's!" she told him. "It was a referral from a buyer I met at a sales call five months ago. I didn't sell him anything. I told him that, considering his needs, he'd be better off buying from our competition. He kept my card. Then he called me yesterday and said a friend of his at SnazzyCo was in the market for new systems. It all fell together from there."

"Right on! Honesty is the best policy, isn't it?"

"That's the truth, Jack."

The neighbor sets up a meeting

"Sounds like things are going well," said Jack's neighbor. "I'm glad to hear about the seminar. Can you get me an invite? I'd like to attend. It's next Thursday morning, isn't it?"

"That's right, and it would be awesome if you could make it."

"My pleasure. Now if you have a few more minutes, there's something else I wanted to talk to you about. Remember my friend who introduced me to *Buyer-Approved Selling*? Well, I spoke to him yesterday, and I have some news: He was speaking with Mike, the book's author. Mike's company is putting on a seminar called Buyer-Approved Selling Excellence, or BASE for short. A buyer from HugeGiantCo is flying in from Michigan to facilitate it. I believe it's on the 19th."

"Very cool," said Jack. "A sales course taught by a buyer!"

"My friend also said that Mike was looking for Fortune-500-type companies to work with, so that he and his company, Approved Publications, could customize *Buyer-Approved Selling* to their needs. Here's Mike's card. I think you should consider calling him for details. Then you might approach BigCo and see if they'd be interested in meeting with Mike when he's in town for the BASE seminar. It could be a good move for you."

A chat with the author of *Buyer-Approved Selling*

"Hello, Jack," said Mike. "Sure, I have a quick minute. Thanks for asking."

"First of all, Mike, I want to tell you how impressed my sales partner and I have been with your book. It's had a tremendous influence on our careers."

"Glad to hear that, Jack! My favorite part of sharing this technology is hearing how much it improves people's lives—not just the sellers', but the buyers', too."

Jack gave Mike a brief rundown on BigCo's industry, and told him that BigCo might be a good candidate for a custom version of *Buyer-Approved Selling*.

"I'll courier you some material that you can pass along to your people," Mike said. "It explains the whole process, and if they're interested in exploring it further, we can schedule a meeting for when I'm in town."

"Thanks, Mike. Our VP of sales will likely be the main decision-maker. It may take him a while to get back to you. He's out of town this week; then when he gets back, we're having an information-based seminar—another idea from your book."

When Jack received Mike's package a few days later, he was pleased to see that it included complementary, signed copies of *Buyer-Approved Selling* for him and Morena.

Jack speaks at the seminar

Brian Stevenson had just introduced him, and Jack felt a surge of confidence. He was prepared. He'd rehearsed his presentation until he thought he was ready. Then he'd videotaped it, which had led to more rehearsal.

The next thing Jack knew, his presentation was over. Three things were clear: He'd enjoyed it, the audience had enjoyed it, and he wanted to do more of them.

Erik approached him afterward. "That was very informative, Jack. Thanks for inviting me. By the way, here's Jorge's card—he's our VP of finance. He'll be expecting your call to set up that meeting with your leasing manager."

"Good presentation, Jack. Well done." It was Jack's neighbor. Jack promptly introduced him to Erik, and mentioned that he was the source of the book that led to their second meeting.

"Ah, yes. Jack told me that you were with G.E. I'd be interested in hearing about that."

Jack excused himself so he could attend to the other prospects and customers he'd invited. He knew it was important to say hello to each of them.

By the end of the evening, Jack felt like he was moving to the next level in his career. It was amazing how making one's self an expert in a niche area could be so effective in bolstering people's perceptions.

The company president, the VP of sales, his manager, and his entire sales team had congratulated him on his presentation. Even the normally-aloof Grant had something positive to say. Maybe he wasn't such a bad guy after all.

Leveraging existing success

The next month's BigCo newsletter had a review of the seminar, with a photo of Jack giving his presentation. Jack promptly copied the page and sent it, along with a letter, to his chamber of commerce. They held monthly workshops on a variety of business topics. In his letter, he suggested that the chamber consider him as a facilitator for a workshop on properly maintaining home and office systems. It was a popular topic the chamber's workshops hadn't addressed.

The chamber said yes. They worked out the details, and Jack conducted his second successful speaking engagement. It generated a sale for him three months later, from an attendee who was a buyer for an accounting firm.

Jack then wrote letters to three trade publications to ask if they would be interested in an article he'd written about system maintenance. He included references to his speaking credentials. One of the publications called him right away. There was a last-minute cancellation; could they run his article in their next issue?

Morena's star on the rise

The day after Jack's article was published, he met Morena in the hallway at BigCo before lunch.

"Well, if it isn't Mr. Expert, the published writer! I imagine you'll be buying lunch, with all the money you made from your article."

"Yeah, if you consider fifty dollars a lot of money." Jack laughed. "But the exposure is the valuable part, of course. I'm getting there, one step at a time. In fact, lunch *is* on me, just to show you my confidence! And speaking of success, I should find out about the MajorAccountCo deal any day now."

"I hope you make that sale and win the trip, Jack. I wish I were going, too."

"What do you mean? You're on track to qualify."

"Jack, I made a decision last night. I told you my brother has been bugging me to work for him instead of—well, as he puts it, 'wasting my talents for a corporate giant.' Well, last night he made me an offer I couldn't refuse. It included ownership in his company, a great pay package, and a new company car. He said he'd often thought about inviting me to work for him, and that my experience here at BigCo convinced him to get serious about it."

"That's really something, Morena—congratulations! Although the selfish part of me wishes you'd stay."

"I have you to thank, Jack. We've both worked hard, but if it weren't for you, I might not have heard about *Buyer-Approved Selling*. You're the first person I've told about this, so keep it quiet, okay? I'm waiting till the end of the day to tell my manager."

"I'll sure miss you, Morena. I'll just have to win two tickets so I can take you along!"

Chapter 10
The Payoff

★

Jack hung up the phone, stunned. He couldn't think clearly. He got up from his desk and walked slowly across the hall to Bart's office.

"Morning, Jack," said Bart. "Hey, is something wrong? You look a bit, uh, dazed."

"I am, Bart. You know that deal I've been after with MajorAccountCo, for 27 new GH749A systems?"

"Of course I do."

"Well, I just heard from Erik. It's not happening."

"Aw, Jack, that's too bad. That sale would've been fantastic for you, and we sure would've liked MajorAccountCo onboard again. But you did a great job, considering what you were up against . . ."

"Hang on, Bart. I said *that* deal wasn't happening. Erik said they just signed a major contract and they're ramping up their expansion." Jack's face broke into a wide grin. "So they don't want 27 systems—they want *37!* On the same terms!"

Bart leapt to his feet. "Whoa, way to go, Jack!" He pumped Jack's hand. "You've done the impossible—*more* than the impossible!"

"Erik wondered if we could still deliver by the 15th. Think we can handle something like that so quickly?"

"Let's drop in on Brian right now and find out. I have a feeling he'll be glad to see us. And you'd better start practicing your hula, Jack—you're going to Hawaii!"

It was nine months' quota in one order, and it put Jack in first place in the company standings. Many congratulations came his way over the next few days. Those he appreciated the most were from Morena and his neighbor.

New wheels: The psychology of affluence

A deal like this came along every couple of years, so it was an event. Brian Stevenson gave Jack and Bart a celebration dinner at one of the town's best restaurants, and invited Jack's entire sales team.

Jack decided it was time to have a car that reflected his confidence and his plans for success. He sold his old Mustang—with its dents, rust, and ripped seats—to a grateful teenager in his neighborhood. To take its place, he leased a brand-new Mercedes.

Jack was convinced of the value of positive reinforcement. He knew that quality suits and a quality car affected how others perceived him, but they did something else that was just as important: They affected how Jack perceived himself.

His only problem was that he had to wait until the first of the month to park his shiny new car in the VIP parking spot.

Curious about Jack's success

"Jack, Bart told me that this was your first sales job," said Brian, as they sat in his VP-sized corner office. "I have to admit, I'd like to know how you've done so well right out of the gate. Even before the MajorAccountCo deal, you were on track for your annual quota. That's something only 15 to 20% of new reps ever achieve. With the MajorAccountCo deal, you're now our number-one rep—and with only six weeks to go before fiscal year-end, it looks like you'll keep that title. Jack, I want to improve performance across the board—and from what I've observed, I think there may be some things our other reps could learn from you. So, how did you do it?"

Jack told Brian how the Buyer-Approved Communication System helped Morena and him get up to speed in record time by showing them how to use "buyer-side" approaches. He described the successful schedule they'd developed, and that they were still using it. As he spoke, he could see the wheels turning in Brian's mind.

Jack suddenly remembered. "And speaking of that, Brian, did you get a chance to look at the package I left with your assistant last week?"

"No, I've been swamped. Being out of the office for a week didn't help either. The emails keep piling up—it's an electronic salt mine over here. But Laura did give me your package. Here it is."

Brian opened the package and found a copy of *Buyer-Approved Selling,* with a letter outlining Mike's proposition for a custom edition of the book for BigCo's industry.

"This looks very interesting. I'll go over it tonight. I like the concept—and considering how it affected your MajorAccountCo deal, I'll be paying close attention."

Morena's last day

"Positive energy radiates from you Morena. You're always smiling and full of life. I have to tell you, it's been an amazing experience working with you. You're one of a kind. I'm going to miss our morning coffees."

"Not completely, you won't. I'll be in the area at least once a week, and when I am, I'll be sure to start here at the coffee shop so we can catch up on things. I'm just sorry I'll miss seeing you accept the Salesperson of the Year award at the Annual General Meeting next month."

"No worries, but maybe you can still attend if your brother gives you the time off. I'm sure BigCo would be okay with it. I'd love for you to be there. Without you, I might never have completed the prep work like the ISPS and the GPOS. Even if I had, there's no way it would have turned out so well. All the role-plays we did, all that work . . . So I have a lot to thank you for—and I have just the right gift for you. How about a ticket to Hawaii and Mexico? It comes with your own room, and all meals. All you have to do is get to the airport. What do you say?"

"Twist my arm, Jack. I'd love to! Wow, what a day. Thanks, Jack, that's a sweet thing for you to do. I can't wait to go—we'll have a blast!"

Interesting news about a case study

Jack was walking back from the company cafeteria when he heard himself being paged. It was Erik from MajorAccountCo.

"Can we meet for lunch sometime this week, Jack? I have something I'd like to show you."

"Sure—how's Thursday at 11:50? We'll beat the lunch lineup. Is the Downtown Deli okay with you?"

When they met, Erik wasted no time getting to the point.

"Jack, when you showed me *Buyer-Approved Selling*, it got me thinking that it would make an interesting case study, something I could write an article about. I called *Corporate Selling Excellence* magazine and asked if they'd be interested in an article about the selling process, using a real-life example. They'd already seen the book and they loved the idea, so we agreed to move forward.

"Jack, you're the example I documented. The editor and I would like to use real company names and real people's names. I got the okay from my company, but I would need written permission from you on behalf of BigCo. Here's a copy of the draft before you answer."

Erik was a good writer. The article was clear, accurate, and punchy. It described the approaches Jack had used, and Erik's reactions. It was interesting reading, because it was real.

"I'd be glad to have my name in it, Erik. I'll ask the brass at BigCo about using the company name, and I'll let you know ASAP."

"Great. Here's a permission form for you. If BigCo approves, please have someone copy it to company letterhead, then sign where it says your name and company name."

How could BigCo say no? The article would make Jack and BigCo look good—very good.

Erik ended the article in a particularly positive way: "If every sales rep communicated the way Jack Fontaine did, the selling profession would be seen in a new light."

Jack mentors a rookie

In his twelfth month on Bart's team, Jack learned that one of his teammates was moving on. Soon a new recruit was in his place, and Jack asked Bart if he could mentor him.

Bernard, the rookie, was excited about being trained by the company's top rep. He took Jack's direction well and was "into a groove" by the fourth week. Jack taught him to design a schedule, and how to use the Buyer-Approved concepts. Jack realized he enjoyed teaching—and as Morena said, he was good at it.

Paging Jack to Brian's office

It was late Friday afternoon. Jack was walking down the hall to the rear parking lot when he heard himself paged. "Jack Fontaine, you're requested at Brian Stevenson's office, please."

"I won't keep you, Jack," said Brian. "I just wanted to let you know that I read Erik's article, and I got the okay to use your name and BigCo's name. That's a great story, my boy; you should be proud.

I'll tell you one thing for sure: After reading the article and the book itself, I'm scheduling a meeting with the author of *Buyer-Approved Selling*."

Mike's seminar

"Great seminar yesterday, Mike," said Jack. "The question-and-answer period at the end was especially good—lots of candid questions from the sales people, and some equally candid answers from Chris, your buyer. I heard a lot of questions I'd want to ask someone like him, the lead buyer for a major company, even if he wasn't right there facilitating the training. It was very informative."

"Thanks, Jack. It was a good day for sure. We had a great turnout, and we got very good ratings and comments on the feedback forms."

"It's impressive how interested these important buyers are in participating in your books and programs, Mike, and how many of their companies have authorized you to use their names."

"Jack, you've probably realized this, but Buyer-Approved sales techniques aren't just in the sellers' interests. They're very much in the interests of the buyers and their companies. They make the buyers' jobs a lot easier, and they help companies get the products and services they really need. Everyone wins."

"Well, let's begin, shall we?" said Brian. Mike guided them through the meeting agenda he had emailed them in advance. He used a meeting planner, like the example in *Buyer-Approved Selling*. It was clear that Mike "walked his talk."

Summarizing the key points

"We're nearly out of time," said Mike, "and I want to summarize the key points to make sure I'm not missing anything. I'll write them out and email them to you as well.

"First, we're moving forward with industry-specific research to create a Standards of Performance Manual for BigCo sales reps. It will be laid out similarly to *Buyer-Approved Selling*, including comments from your own customers.

"Marketshare Research Institute will interview fifty BigCo customers to determine the top approaches they would like your sales reps to use consistently. We'll use the current book as a checklist for them to select from, and add any new approaches or procedures they recommend. That, by the way, is how we keep *Buyer-Approved Selling* on the cutting edge. Sales is an evolving field, and we never intend to stop updating our material.

"Once the fifty customer interviews are complete, you have the option of having us interview some non-customers as well, to see if we can learn why they don't currently deal with you. As you know, our research shows that they're more likely to tell a third party how they really feel.

"Finally, we've agreed on a price for an initial order of 100 books for your reps, and a reorder price. Is there anything else you can think of?"

"There is one more thing. If we want to have your people come in for custom sales training based on the Standards of Performance you develop, would that be possible?"

"Absolutely. I would have brought it up myself, but at this point I didn't want to inundate you with too many options. Our sister company, Approved Learning Inc., could handle that."

"Appreciated," said Brian. "Let's see how the Standards of Performance turn out."

A peek into BigCo's future

Four months later, the Standards of Performance were distributed to the BigCo sales department, and Approved™ Learning sent in trainers to conduct Buyer-Approved Selling Excellence (BASE) workshops. The efficiently-structured training sessions got the reps up to speed quickly and effectively, and the new selling process helped Jack's branch of BigCo produce more sales than ever before.

The improved numbers got some attention at BigCo HQ. When they learned that the Buyer-Approved Communication System had increased sales revenue by 18% in the first quarter alone, they reviewed it and decided to roll it out nationally. By licensing the training from Approved Learning Inc., they were able to use their own trainers to conduct the workshops.

Over the years, BigCo developed a new and improved reputation. They became known as good communicators—a big company that used personal touches such as the Advanced Meeting Agenda; the email summary of key points; and clear, concise voice mail. Dealing with BigCo's sales reps became a predictable experience for their customers, and they rewarded it with loyalty.

Erik's article: A catalyst for change

The president of MajorAccountCo was on the phone with Erik.

"Erik, I read your article about your dealings with BigCo. That was a good idea. I want to confirm something: You said that the Buyer-Approved sales methods made your job easier, and therefore had a positive influence on sales—yet most reps who called on us rarely used them. Is that correct?"

"It's true, Ted, unfortunately. Take the Advance Meeting Agenda for example. Maybe 10% of the reps send them."

"How would you like it if 100% of them did? I'm thinking of a new policy that will require *every* visiting sales rep to send an agenda before meeting with any of our staff. What do you think?"

"You know how I'd feel about that. And it'll be simple to manage, Ted. If they don't send an agenda, we don't meet with them. While we're on the subject, there are a few other approaches I'd like to include in that policy. May I email you my list?"

"Perfect—send it over. We'll see how it matches mine. Once we've identified the new requirements, I'll have my EA send a letter to all our suppliers. We can direct new suppliers to our website and they'll be able to download the new policy."

The new rules made Erik's job easier and increased his department's productivity. The meeting agendas allowed shorter meetings with increased focus on planned objectives. He never hesitated to require reps to follow these guidelines; it made them more efficient. Some of them started using the tools with their other prospects. It was just good business.

Aloha, Jack and Morena

Jack reclined his seat and put on his headphones to watch the in-flight movie. It would be another four hours before they landed in Honolulu, and Morena was fast asleep beside him, her head on his shoulder.

Jack found it hard to focus on the movie. He kept thinking about that incredible moment the previous month, at the company's AGM, when he was called up to the stage to accept the Salesperson Of The Year award. He hadn't felt nervous—he'd felt proud. He'd worked hard to reach that moment. In his speech, he thanked Morena and his neighbor, and said he'd never have gone so far without their help. When he finished, they were first in line to congratulate him.

The Neighbor's Wisdom

- "When you meet someone in business, don't say 'How are you?' It sounds insincere . . . That's exactly what you expect a sales rep to say."
- "Learn from existing excellence, or invent mediocrity."
- "A good leader praises others when things go right, and accepts the blame when things go wrong. Humility is the key."
- "Always identify and examine the flip-side of every business decision."
- "It makes sense to ask people if they have a minute to talk, especially since you're calling them unsolicited. "
- "The reps who were prepared, and who used common courtesy, always had a better chance with me."
- [On asking for the prospect's permission to proceed with a cold call] "It says the caller is sensitive about the prospect's time. That implies professionalism. And if the rest of the call is structured and to-the-point, it supports that perception."
- [On booking appointments well in advance] "Perception is reality. It's important to create the perception that you're a busy sales rep whose time is in demand."
- "Whenever possible, be one minute early for a business meeting."
- [On initial meetings] "Let friendship come later. Insincere small talk is just a variation on the 'How are you?' approach . . . People buy from people they trust. When

you get down to business, and you're helpful and easy to deal with, that's a great start."

- "When you listen, you do more than give your prospect a chance to speak. You show the prospect that you're really interested in their needs, that you're not just trying to 'sell' them. Communication is a two-way street—and that means listening is an essential skill."
- "A businessperson might consider walking a bit faster than average. Not so you look like you're running late, but so you look like someone with a purpose."
- "Join your local chamber of commerce."
- [On the importance of making contacts] "'It's not who you know—it's who knows you.'"
- "Effective networking isn't just a matter of showing up, shaking a few hands, and exchanging a few business cards. It's like anything: You can do it well or poorly, and the results speak for themselves."
- "There's a fine line between annoying people and keeping in touch with them."
- "You can judge someone's character by how they treat the waiter."
- "Winners never quit, and quitters never win."

About the Author

Michael Schell spent 20 years in business-to-business sales, primarily in highly-competitive, commission-based industries, where he won numerous achievement awards. Michael is President and CEO of the Approved Group of Companies in Vancouver, British Columbia, including:

Approved Publications Inc.

(www.approvedpublicationsinc.com)

Approved Learning Inc.

(www.approvedlearninginc.com)

Marketshare Research Institute

(www.marketshareresearch.com)

When Michael isn't writing books, appearing as a keynote speaker, or working with his talented staff, he enjoys cycling, traveling, playing guitar with his rock band, and jumping out of perfectly good airplanes.

About The Approved™ Series

During his corporate sales career, author Michael Schell attended many sales seminars and workshops. He read hundreds of books on sales, business development, public speaking, and human relations. He often wondered:

- Why did sales authors and speakers take so much time to explain simple concepts, and to describe specific, practical ways to use them?
- How did the methods they recommended work in the real world?
- Where was the validation from the people who mattered most: the buyers?

Mike realized that the book he was looking for had not been written—a book from the perspective of the people who were *sold to*. These people had met and interacted with countless sales reps; they knew exactly what worked and what didn't. Who could explain selling better than professional buyers?

The result was *Buyer-Approved Selling*, a book filled with practical, no-nonsense approaches recommended by buyers from many companies across the U.S. This groundbreaking book has been embraced by the corporate community. Some businesses have ordered custom editions of it for their sales departments.

Mike has been invited to lead special **Buyer-Approved training workshops** and is in demand as a keynote speaker. Backed by the Approved Series's extensive research and his own first-hand knowledge of sales, Mike presents the Buyer-Approved sales concepts in a concrete, ready-to-use form that sales professionals can immediately apply to their work.

How the Approved Series works for you

The Approved Series focuses on the opinions of the decision-makers who are most important to you and your work:

You	Decision-makers	Approved Series Title
Sales representative	Professional buyers	*Buyer-Approved Selling*
Small-business owner	Corporate customers	*The Customer-Approved Small Business*
Job seeker	Employers	*Human Resource-Approved Job Interviews & Resumes*

Each Approved Series book gives you a complete step-by-step plan for achieving the results you seek, based on advice from the kinds of people you want to influence. In addition to the recommended methods, you'll read decision-makers' actual comments as they explain why some methods work and some fail. (The answers may surprise you!)

It's one thing to read a book and another to apply it. You can use the Approved Series with confidence, knowing that its techniques come from "the right side of the desk." It makes all the difference!